To Alan

With much love

Barbara & Philip

12/5/07

CLASSIFICATION: POETRY

A CIP catalogue record for this book is available from
the British Library.

Printed and bound in Great Britain.

Paper used in the production of books published by
United Press comes only from sustainable forests.

This North West of England and Northern Ireland edition

ISBN 978-1-84436-522-7

First published in Great Britain in 2007 by
United Press Ltd
Admail 3735
London
EC1B 1JB
Tel: 0870 240 6190
Fax: 0870 240 6191
ISBN for complete set of volumes
978-1-84436-528-9
All Rights Reserved

www.unitedpress.co.uk

Home Thoughts

Foreword

One of the great joys of my job is handing out £1,000 prizes to winners of our poetry competitions.

That joy has now magnified because we have doubled the number of prize competitions we run. Our first cash competition, The National Poetry Anthology, is now almost a decade old. Poems for this competition have to be submitted by June 30th every year.

As with all the competitions we run, entries must be no more than 20 lines and no more than 160 words, but each poet is allowed to submit up to three entries.

The fact that this competition is completely free contrasts refreshingly with modern trends in poetry. All the other big competitions charge entry fees which are now rising to around £7 per poem. This would mean that entrants who sent three poems to another competition would have to send £21, and their chances of winning against so many thousands of other poets are very slim indeed.

The National Poetry Anthology has become so successful that last year we decided to launch a new competition with an annual closing date of December 31st.

This competition is for poets to submit up to three poems, with the same length limitations, on a specific subject. We asked them to write about someone or something linked to their home town.

Since we started running that competition we've received some really excellent poetry. I have always felt that poems written from personal experience are better than any other kind of poem.

And I think this competition and the poems selected for this book prove that fact. There is no better example than the 2007 winner of the £1,000 cash prize Marjorie Beachill of Wath-upon-Dearne.

Marjorie has only just become a UK citizen. She was born and lived most of her life in Hawaii. "I came to Wath nine years ago," explained Marjorie. "A new man entered my life and because I loved him so much I travelled half way across the world to be with him." Marjorie and husband John are happily settled in Wath.

Marjorie's poem stood out for us as touching, affectionate, from the heart and very endearing. She has obviously fallen in love not just with John, but with the whole village.

Lynda Brennan, Editor

MY VILLAGE

If there's one thing you'll learn
From Wath-upon-Dearne
It's just how a village should be.

You can take any path,
Queen of villages, Wath
England's beauty is right here to see.

For what once was the goal
To mine enough coal
Built a people of vitality.

And now I look around
From my house to the town
And am glad to live here and be me.

For from Hadrian's Wall
To the tip of Cornwall
I have travelled for many a day.

Round the world I have flown
Many villages known
But when asked I can honestly say.

I shall always return to Wath-upon-Dearne
To my village, my heart's final stay.

Marjorie Beachill, Wath-upon-Dearne

Contents

The poets who have contributed to this volume are listed below, along with the relevant page upon which their work can be found.

71	Rachel Van Den Bergen	107	Susan Lord
	Alan Withers	108	Carole Lawrence
72	Arnold Harrison	109	Ian Clayton
73	Heather Kaye	110	Barbara Hartley
74	Ken Bradbury Harrop	111	Stephen John Davidson
75	Joyce Torkington	112	Pam Dixon
76	Katie Haigh	113	Bill Austin
77	Kathleen Frances West		Dean Wakefield
78	Jennifer Starkie	114	Cecil E Beach
	Doris Turner	115	Christine Dickinson
79	Kathleen Hinks	116	Elva Knott
80	John T Boardman		Claire Cookson
81	Billal Mahmood	117	Valerie Smith
82	Sean Harewood	118	Stephen Alan Greasley
83	Samuel Fisher	119	Bob Harrison
84	Sylvia Lee	120	Donald Armitage
85	Graham Scotson	121	Joseph Alston
	Louise Gillard	122	Holly White
86	Irene McWillam	123	Allan Dixon
87	Lilian Lines	124	Isaac Livesey
88	Carol-Anne Wheelton	125	Albert Penty
	Janice Cheetham	126	Gina Riley
89	Ian Aitchison	127	Libby Grimes
90	Jean Flatters	128	Geoffrey W Lever
91	Denise Wild	129	Marie Keating
92	Margaret Fox	130	Marie Smith
93	Frank Warren	131	Vincent McNicholas
94	Taylor Coppell	132	Jean Emmett
	Doreen Baggaley	133	John B Townsley
95	Sandra Jones	134	Marjorie Riding
96	Ian Stone		Sheila Harper
97	Linda Flynn	135	Barbara Robinson
98	Eve Ingham	136	Ben Lee Almond
99	Eric Tomlinson	137	Nancy Reeves
100	Eva Smith	138	Joanne Platt
101	Shirley C Daniels	139	Glenway
102	June Plaskett	140	Jean Turner
103	Derek Pepperdine	141	Kara Walmsley
104	Shirley Pinnington	142	Barrie Whittaker
105	Teresa Gethings	143	Roy Hawkes
106	Patricia Bamber		Ena Barker
		144	Jake Jackson

	Kenneth Houghton		Jane Bazley-Harrison
146	Dorothy Ellis	183	Philip Rowe
147	John Neil Ruffley	184	Melanie Robinson
148	Maureen O'Hara	185	Ross Bagnall
149	Andrea Blease		Brenda Marshman
150	Keith Clegg	186	Susan Mansell
151	Eileen Naylor	187	Marie Black
152	Timothy Cunningham	188	Adam Scanlon
153	Jack Lindon		Andrea Rollins
154	Ron Sen	189	Pauline Williams
155	Joan Pyrke	190	Carole Ginty
156	Brian Williams	191	Anna Hindmarch
	Trevor Jones	192	Ann Tregenza
157	Andrew Smith	193	Dorothy Gerrard
158	Brian Lally	194	Ian Dorrington
159	Jean Jones	195	Kenneth Thompson
160	Graham Collum	196	Gillie Bishop
	Judith Hinds	197	Rosemary Osa Quirke
161	Matthew Jung	198	Edward Marriette
162	Carol Houghton	199	Rosemary Critchley
163	Diane Horscroft	200	Shauna Grant
164	Peter Jones	201	Fiona J Finegan
165	Leila Rooney	202	Patrick Gormley
166	Thomas Minhsull	203	Joseph Mullan
167	Les Woods	204	Vincent Breen
168	Frankie Shepherd	205	Mark Long
	Sally-Ann Davies	206	Julie Parker
169	Jackie Marsh	207	Keith Watson
170	Joan Rawcliffe	208	Harry Press
171	Thomas McCabe	209	Georgina Wright
	Gabriel McNeilly	210	Anna McBrien
172	Lucy Sellars	211	Emma Murray
173	Ronald A Crabtree	212	Winston Graydon
174	Wendy Black	213	Shirley Gault
175	Julien Toh	214	Rhonda Todd
	Rose Maher		Aimee Hislop
176	Paddy McCarty	215	Gillian Ewing
177	Andrew C Chapman	216	Paul Wilkinson
178	Dorothy Crossley	217	Florence Bradshaw
179	Emma Richardson	218	Raymond Meenagh
180	Janet Ashton	219	Regina McLaughlin
181	Joan Jackson	220	Joan C Fyvie
182	Albert Carpenter	221	John Matthew

9

	Jamison
222	Bernadette Kevin
223	Betty McIlroy
	Joan MacCabe
224	Daniel Shaw
225	William Donaldson
226	Elizabeth Aulds
227	Mona Sharkey
228	Olive Thompson
229	Pauline Herbison
230	Marian McGrath
231	Margaret Smyth
	Charlene Ramsey
232	Sharon Proctor
233	Jean Gardner
234	Kittie Carr
235	Ella Stirling
236	Natalia Tochenykh
237	Peggy Galloway
238	Sally Evans

MEMORIAL HALL REMEMBERED

I went to see the Rolling Stones
When they were singing *Satisfaction*
Bought tickets for the Merseybeats
They were billed as the main attraction
I even saw Roy Orbison
When he was singing *Blue Bayou*
But I never saw the Beatles
When they were singing *She Loves You*

I think I saw Paul Simon once
Homeward Bound from Northwich station
It was very late on Friday night
So I could have been mistaken
I once shook hands with Billy J
And met Unit Four Plus Two
But I never saw the Beatles
When they were singing *She Loves You*

Philip Dennis

SPRING HEELED JACK

Spring heeled Jack, now there's a mystery,
that infamous character, went down in history.
He could leap over houses, with the greatest of ease,
jump over rivers and even tall trees.
He was seen in Warrington, my home town,
not knocking on doors in his dressing gown,
but leaping over houses in Horsemarket Street,
then he jumped Central Station in one giant leap.
That was in nineteen twenty, a long time ago,
when Jack frightened people, with his own one man show.
But I wonder what became of spring heeled Jack,
maybe he was followed by two *men in black,*
because one theory is, he was from outer space,
with his fiery eyes and his fearsome face.
So if you're on Central Station, or Horsemarket Street,
be aware, because you don't know who you might meet.
Spring heeled Jack, may be waiting, to give you a fright,
before laughing, then leaping off into the night.

Christopher Taylor

NORTHWICH

There are lots of nice old buildings
In Northwich where I live
They're timber framed and painted black and white
The only thing that spoils us
Is the traffic on the roads
I wish the council folk could get it right
There is a lot of water
Rivers and canals
Where you can take a boat ride
Or go fishing with your pals
There are lots of friendly people
And places you can sit
And lovely parks and woodland
You can walk round if you're fit
We have a lot of history
The boat lift just for one
And don't forget the good old salt
That we are built upon

Barbara Prescott

AM I LOCAL OR LOCO?

I asked myself, when I came to write this poem
Am I local or loco or maybe both?
After all I live here and I work for the local mental health
trust
A conundrum or just a humdrum question
Whatever! That's the way to answer
Which is, of course, no answer at all
After all I wasn't born here and I didn't start my career
here either
So maybe I'm neither local nor loco
I'm sure most people don't care one way or the other
Until of course the pigeons come home to roost so to speak
Then of course it becomes the most important question of
all time
When these things involve yours truly
Local or loco is not just a conundrum or a humdrum
question anymore
It's, am I local or loco?

                                                    Tim Caton

POP HORNBY

What a lovely time to look back
All those years ago.
Where young lovers used to meet
And folk just seemed to know.

Pop Hornby was the owner and friend
All the regulars met in there.
His *herb shop* was the greatest
And the drinks made with loving care.

Plaza cinema was near at hand
Where a night out was in mind.
Romance was in great demand
Where dates were made and planned.

Maybe Pop could see it all
At the counter where he stood.
Just fancy all those soft drinks.
And the lives he touched with love.

Edith Cooke

SALT

The bleary eyed men are busy at night
As the whole of the country turns shimmering white
The frosty cold seeps into their bones
They are busy talking on their mobile phones
We need more salt to lay on the roads
To stop skids, accidents and lost loads
Thank goodness for salt from its Cheshire source
Without it the country would stop of course
At Winsford a magical underground world
A hive of activity as the precious salt is hurled
Into trucks large and bulky with tyres so big
Then up to the surface they come from the big dig
Out to those men on the country's white highway
Making sure users are safe, local and far away

Janet Glover

NORTHWICH

Welcome to Northwich, a beautiful town,
It's graceful and historic, we won't let you down.
Lovely sights to see and people to meet,
So come on down to Northwich - get up on your feet.

Come and see our salt museum, there are lots of things to
do.
If you want history we will bring it right to you.

Our local park is Marbury it is such a delight,
We take our dogs for walks there, it is a wonderful sight.

There is also the Anderton boat lift it is famous through
and through,
Come and have a day here and you can see it too.

Perri Rowe

TEAR

No ear could hear, no words could say
The way I felt there on that day
Yet came there none, those silver tears
Of grief, to me and of my fears.

Just silently I sat and shook
Expressionless but for the look
In my eyes as out I stared
Into the world for which I cared.

Somehow my grief it seemed concealed
Not again to be revealed
Yet swept away clean out of sight
Like the silent moth on a windy night.

No word escaped my lips that day
To tell a soul I felt that way
Emotion is not meant to hide
Be bottled up and swept aside.

Christopher Johnson

WHERE LOVE IS

When orphaned I came to live
in the old *manse* gas lit and drab, but spring
woke beauty that only the country can give
and across the lane a skylark would sing.
Escaping the *manse* I'd turn down the lane
watching clog footed girls clatter past.
A sight not often seen again
because the old salt mine was closing at last.

Then the Wharton *manse* was sold,
gas light removed as the country receded.
The house soon admired because it was old
attracted new buyers when needed.

I should have learned from years long gone,
the *manse* was always a hard house to leave.
But I tried to care, though love hate held on,
I tried to care, so I wouldn't grieve one
who loved his home with a love deep and strong.

Margaret Hoole

CHESHIRE TREASURE

From the Golden Arrow, to the A Four Pacific.
Rolls Royce and Bentley, this town is prolific.
A match for the best, our park is a beautiful sight.
We have Britannia, The Alexandra and The Limelight.

Our girls are caring, happy and pretty wonderful.
Let's say I'm given one word to describe them, irresistible.
The men are steadfast and true to Crewe.
Humourous and hot blooded, ask the girls they woo.

Strangers are coming, looking for a new future.
Searching for work, embracing our culture.
Why not work as a team, try to blend in.
And if we are successful, everyone will win.

Wanderers by nature, my friends and I love to roam.
But there's warmth in our hearts, when we head home.
Time to bring to heel, those boring grey suits.
For we love Crewe, here lie our roots.

Michael Malam

THE NORTHWICH WINGS CLUB BINGO NIGHT

We play bingo at our club
You can get a drink like a pub
It doesn't cost a lot to play
And most people till the end will stay
The caller likes a bit of fun
He's a laugh and makes your eyes run
Each week it's the same old faces
And they all sit in the same places
Every week some people will win
And they collect their winnings with a grin
Some people don't like others to win
They think it's a sin
Sometimes they leave the extractor fan on
You may miss a number it could have gone
While playing the game the glass collector is walking about
The bingo caller might not hear you shout
If somebody wins the jackpot game
You will hear the caller shout out their name
At the end of the night it's been fun
Even if you have not won

Eric Barratt

CHESHIRE

Cheshire is our heritage,
A special place to dwell,
Our county holds much treasure,
As history books will tell.

Churches and castles, old as the hills,
Caves and cathedrals, old water mills,
Ruins and landscapes, views so serene,
Lakes and woodlands, rivers and streams.

The Saxons and Romans all passed this way,
But for most Cheshire dwellers,
The hearts are here to stay.

Edith Shaw

WHERE I LIVE IS SECRET

Where I live is secret,
That's how it has to be,
For, if this secret should get out,
Who knows who might visit me
And I'd get asked lots of questions
And be told of far off places
Which are supposed to mean something to me,
But which are as strange as all their faces.
I couldn't go through that again,
It's traumatic and it's tiring.
They think they are so clever and cute,
But they don't know I know they're conspiring
To prise from me my worldly goods
And so the last laugh will be mine,
They can't reach me where I'm living now,
They would have to reach inside my mind!

Michael J Parsons

A SHORT STEP FROM HOME

A gate post clad with ivy
On which hangs a rusty five bar gate
Overgrown and almost hidden
Secured in place with twine,
The autumn sun dying embers glow
Glints upon the polished plough
Gulls that all day followed
Flock, then head away to roost,
A new born calf unsure of foot
Attempts first time to suckle
Encouraged by a mother's gentle love,
In a barn stacked full
Of sweet scented meadow hay
An owl stares, then blinks
Stretching out its silent wings.
The old oak adorned
In golden autumn glory
Stands steadfast against the winter winds
Whilst the mist still lingers over
The distant Pennine way.

Frank Watson

THE GARDEN SHED

My garden shed is dead
And that's all that can be said.
For years it stood in the corner by the hedge
Between the flower border and the veg.
Its wooden sides have rotted and decayed
The door won't shut and the roof felt is frayed.
My jilted son whose broken tender teenage heart
Crouched in a corner sobbing, grieving, his whole world
torn apart.
I myself found refuge when my mother died
I just stood there and at last I cried and cried,
Finding solace in this familiar place
A constant in our world of changing face.
Our much loved cat went missing for a day,
We found her curled around her kittens in a seedling tray.
Mothering, licking, suckling, purring so loud,
Guarding her babies, so right, natural and proud.
Throughout the shed's life it has been a place
Where family members have found a private space.
And now it's gone - it served us well
Old friend - farewell!

Margaret Cann

LIVERPOOL, CAPITAL OF THE UNIVERSE

Through the sunshine, through the rain,
Through the window, through the pain,
Painting pictures inside my brain.
I've touched the soul of Liverpool,
Now I long to take you there,
Two cages with lions in,
One called Bush and one called Blair.
It's dinner time!

Church without a roof reflecting the blitz, swamped in
misery,
Stories I've read and heard,
The Everton roar, the Liverpool cheer,
Come on you reds, come on you blues
Get them cobwebs off your dancing shoes.
I've witnessed the future, visited the past,
A magical journey I pray will last.
Bring back the heroes, bring back them all
Lennon, Harrison, Ringo, Sir Paul.
Miles and miles of smiles shall guide you on your way.
A warm friendly embrace awaits you all in Liverpool today.

Steven Kenyon

THE FROZEN NORTH

Steel and stone and old cold days,
bricks and bones and sing-song bays,
where the water flows
and the tide is rising
till tomorrow shows.

I'm wintering out,
in an early dark,
walking with the wind
in November's park.

This town is something
out of a force ten storm,
the streets are shivering
in the frozen north.

And it's sharp
with ice and
cold as snow,
and the world is shaking
in the gales as they blow.

Michael Jones

GONE BUT NOT FORGOTTEN

Sitting on the train, I travelled back in time
To my home town, of coal smoking chimneys and grime
Everyone did a hard days work, to buy their daily bread
Wages bought no luxuries, just kept their families fed.
Everybody knew everybody, and their business too
One community, one spirit, one point of view
The smell of freshly baked bread, floated through the narrow streets
Ready to accompany a plate of stew, with very little meat.
Children content playing with their marbles and spinning tops
No computers or mobile phones, yet happy with their lot
Public houses filled with laughter and the tinkling of ivory keys
Men discussing, debating the issues in which they believed.
Hospitality lived behind every terraced door
A welcoming fire, hot teapot, who needed more
Facing life and death, standing side by side
A small town, big on respect and pride.
Goodbye reality, I'm staying in the past
When daily living, was a pleasurable task.

Denise Baines

THROUGH MY WINDOW

As I look through my window
With its window frame
I see lots of trees
They're not all the same

In the spring they begin to grow
And soon their leaves and blossom show

In the summertime they look just fine
When the sun begins to shine

In the autumn the leaves they fall
Tumbling down one and all

In the winter they look so bare
But when it snows
The branches bring a magic to the air

It's then that I realise
That my window, with its window frame
Is really an ever changing picture
And picture frame

Margaret Hicks

MEMORIES OF QUEENS PARK, CREWE

From Victorian times to the present day
Queens Park is the place to play
Games to play, ice-cream to share
For young and old there's something there
Birds, boats and bands too
Yes, there's always things to do
Swings and roundabouts, sometimes a fair
Fishing, bowls with a bit of flair
Picnics under the cherry tree
Bring back happy memories to me

Hazel M Finch

LOCAL PRIDE

Singing songs of local pride,
In the shadows more locals hide.

He took out his weapon,
Thinks he's on a roll,
Tongues and feet kicked through his soul.

Morning comes,
Local papers arrive,
Last night somebody local died.

We knew it was bad,
We knew danger was near,
But we never thought it would happen here.

Soon more bad news the papers bring,
Is this the pride of which we sing?

Gemma Connell

WHAT A TOWN

What a town
Full of ash and lime,
Salt and grime chimneys,
Steam and smoke.
Some time ago folk
Would choke, but now things
Are clean basically a dream.
Rivers, lakes and fields of green,
A canal passes through with
Barges and boats passing fields
Of oats. Farmers in tractors,
Collecting grain before the
Autumn rain. It may all
Seem insane but this is what
We gain. The Industrial age
Has gone and now we're free
From all that smog and muck.
Go down to the river and
Feed a swan or a duck. Walk
In the park, go out after dark,
Feel free to breathe, but,
Remember you must never
Leave Northwich town.

Jeffrey Harradine

OUR TOWN, CREWE

This is a poem of our town Crewe
Places to see and lots to do
A walk in the park amongst the trees
Smelling the flowers, and the humming of bees

Our railway station is one of the best
From north, south, east and west
We had a visit from the Duke and the Queen
That was the best sight we have ever seen

Plenty of pubs to have a few beers
Crewe works has been here many a year
It's no longer the famous *Rolls Royce*
Now it's *Bentley* the car of your choice

Crewe Alex is our local football team
To win the cup would be a dream
We have a carnival with floats every year
People lining the streets ready to cheer

The Britannia statue stands very proud
Where people lay their wreaths around the ground
Great restaurants and different places to eat
Lots of shops where we can all meet

Patricia Henshall

CHESTER, THE QUEEN BEE

I saw you and fell in love instantly
You are like a living history book
You are a jewel with faces of plenty
You are a city with changing looks

You are a stunning masterpiece, which glows
Full of delightful surprises
With your crowning glory, the Rows
Two shopping levels, it's a retail bliss

Roman legions, loved you too
They named you *Deva* the dazzling
City walls, amphitheatre, tombstones
Everything leaves us fascinating

Your cathedral, Eastgate clock
Old building with faces of the past
A haven of reflective tranquillity
In a cosmopolitan centre bustling lively

Your great treasure like the racecourse
And on the beautiful river Dee
Pleasure boats and swans glide effortlessly
Chester, with any doubt you are the queen bee

Victorine Lejeune-Stubbs

SANDBACH MARKET SQUARE

Cobbles revealed,
Car parking no more,
The crosses stand
Tall and majestic,
Tell us such tales,
Reveal Saxon life.
Enjoy the space
Now created here.
Beautiful square
All should now enjoy.

Angela Pritchard

NORTHWICH

I remember walking the rainy streets of Northwich,
The Christmas lights make you feel warmer as you walk for
the bus
From our house there was a chimney horizon,
The ICI smoke and you knew you were home.
I remember the blue balls next to the river,
Next to the river my *nan* fell into when she was a young
girl.

I remember football on concrete
Under grey Rudheath skies
Late for my tea, I remember the lies.

I remember the market
On particular days
The smell of fresh fruit on long Saturdays.

Green buses, stood waiting
It's Somerfield now
I remember those days as if they were now.

With the charm of the folk
You're never alone
I've left Northwich now, but I still call it home.

David Lee

A COUNTY TOWN

Strolling up the High Street of a county town,
Watching all the world go passing up and down.
There goes the lame boy who's dressed in old blue jeans:
To ride a motorcycle is one of his dreams.

See the old lady wearing a puzzled frown,
With the weight of shopping bags pulling her down;
The dizzy blonde goes with her head in the clouds;
An errand boy on his bike whistling out loud.

Bright as a button is Andy, tho' deaf and dumb;
Farmer James - a solid man - smiles a welcome.
Clutching his stick is the gentle Mr Cassis,
And a prim lady looks over her glasses.

The lady with the flowers on her best hat,
Suddenly she stops to have a little chat;
The sun shines down on lovely lads and lasses,
Whilst the traffic up and down it still passes.

Doctor John strides out in his deer-stalker hat;
Mrs Rafferty waddles, jolly and fat;
Beautiful scents - and sometimes obnoxious smells;
But who would want to change this for all the oil wells?

J. Millington

DRUID ECHOES

When asked what stirs me about this place;
It is not the beauty or the grace,
But the pride I feel each misty dawn,
As I stand upon the shores of Ynys Môn.

The seabirds cry above my head.
The wind whispers the secrets of the dead.
The sand beneath my feet gives way,
As I hear the echoes of that distant day.

I share their pain as their warriors fought,
Protecting the magical knowledge the Romans sought.
Not one word or parchment found,
Their secrets safe absorbed by sacred ground.

The silence of the slain defeated the Empire that day,
Even though they had killed the Druid Way.
The blood of my ancestors flowed to earth;
The magical knowledge had been given re-birth.

As I stand upon the shores of Ynys Môn today
I cannot read the words of that ancient way,
But listen, renewed through nature's song.
This Druid is taught by my mother's tongue.

Robert Dickinson

HEREITH

The call of Wales.
Its Celtic soul, stunning beauty.
The mountains beckon the prodigals back to the homeland.
And they come,
Slowly, but surely.
My Yorkshire man is unyielding.
Yet still, I nibble away.
We're going to view a Welsh property tomorrow.
Fingers crossed.

Rachel Bayliss

MACCLESFIELD

Many hills look down on Macc
And the wasp on my glass keeps coming back.
Sat outside *The Society Rooms*
There's a silk museum with quiet looms.

Above, the moving July skies
And people queue for *Spearings* pies.
Hairdressers and charity shops,
The silk road traffic never stops.

Tired legs on Church Street brew
A football team that plays in blue.
Mads Theatre drama or laugh
Heroes names at the cenotaph.

And still many hills look down on Macc
And the wasp on my glass keeps coming back.

Fred B Doherty

ON THE ROAD TO WERNETH LOW

Dear Occupier, we must re-surface
All the roads surrounding your place,
To be done and cleared away
Within six weeks of starting day.

It began. The workmen showed up,
Launched on months of digging road up.
Well entrenched, no more to roam,
They now call these environs home.

Here within their shabby huts
A parallel lifestyle abuts
Complete with their own eco-system,
Have their families not missed 'em?

Indigenous, they now emerge
From hedgerow or a roadside verge,
Although not one of them was born a
Member of our local fauna.

I asked how long their stay would be,
The wistful answer, *you tell me.*
And as I left the plea rang out
If you should hear, give us a shout.

Shirley Brierley

WHITE NANCY

Beacon of light - empress of life - you ever watch over us all.
Maiden in time - guardian of peace - you once blessed Napoleon's fall.
New colours unfurled in your spectral dawn
Your constancy reigns from whence you were borne
Quarries of stone - steep sloping fields - they heed now your vernal call.

Summerhouse pure from Ingersley Hall - you oversee all of our plight.
Landmark of grace - imperial love - this Pennine fringe takes to flight.
Bollinbrook's haze over millponds on fire
Blaze Hill meandering higher and higher
Gardens in bloom - solstice sustaining and hailing your heavenly sight.

Middlewood Way's pre industrial lore - remembers the age of steam.
Canalside community's mills and town houses recapture the days that have been.
Sacristans, acolytes, prayers from the spires
Sepulchres, sanctuaries, festival choirs
Forever our keeper, our symbol, protector; the lady of whom we all dream.

Philip John Savage

THE RIVER DEE

Flowing gently on its course, slowly, silent, without force,
springing from Wales Bala Lake, leaving hamlets in its
wake;
'neath varied skies - many sounds, leading to the city
bounds;
Tractors, aeroplanes, a car: changing landscape by the
hour.

Campanologistic bells; driftwood carried on its swells.
Huntington set to its right; Boughton too comes into sight;
swinging left beside Queens Park, still outpouring in the
dark.
Passes calmly through the Groves - soon the weir its course
behoves.

Skirting now the city walls - under Handbridge, as it falls -
with racecourse north; golf club south, hasting on towards
its mouth.
Maybe gives a sigh, a snort, seeing there its disused port.
Chester's Dee has long served man:- long 'ere Romans
came, it ran.

Nowadays, boats, yachts abound. From its waters comes
the sound
of coxless fours, single skulls; mingling with some
screeching gulls.
Water cruisers play their part; closely linked to Chester's
heart.
Focal point for all to see - Cestrians love the River Dee

Frederick Davies

WORDS

How many words in this word, of *Macclesfield* can you see?
Because Macclesfield's a special word
as it mean *home* to me.

A lively place with lots of space for folks like me and you.
You won't be bored, so be assured
there's lots for you to do.

Amid the fields a bustling town, where friends enjoy a
meal.
To meet and greet in cafe shops
where business deals are sealed.

A market square, a church stands there, a town where
plans are made.
To welcome friends and families
as foundation stones are laid.

Among the shops you'll find a Mall, inside a good food hall.
You'll also find a smiley face
with nice things on the stall.

Two minutes to the countryside, for walks I'll often go.
Then wander round the narrowboats,
calm water, life is slow.

Such lovely words of Macclesfield are written every year
So how many words in *Macclesfield* can your readers see
in here?

Elaine Heywood

MACCLESFIELD

Macclesfield. Born out of the black
Earth of East Cheshire, cradled in
The valley like a sleeping child.
Awakening to the cry of industry
At first light. With dark sullen faces
Trapped in their silken web.

David Farr

THE BAKERY

I wake up in the dead of night,
rub my eyes and open up my window,
the smell of which my nose does greet,
brings a smile to my lips, and for my
stomach a delicious treat.
Freshly baked bread I could just
take-away drifts across to my room
from Roberts Bakery.

Aaron Woodhead

GUIDING SPIRIT

Middlewich! Intriguing town, centre of our county.
Just middling geographically tho' - it yields *enormous*
bounty.

Unassuming it may appear, mere dot on Cheshire plain.
But! Don't cross it off too carelessly, or 'spell' it with
disdain.

For, between two other *wiches,* a sort of civic sorcerer
resides
Who works mysterious magic - on the people, who he
guides.

A wizard, inspiring townsfolk to discover with delight
The rich and complex history of this habitation site.

Here locals combine copiously to harness heritage all can
share.
Then, it's public celebration! They put on a great big fair.

This spirit of community pervades the very streets it seems.
With anti-litter prong and bag, they'll prowl the place in
teams.

A town which pulls together then, clean, informed and
proud.
Mystic sorcerer at large perhaps? Or just a damn good
crowd.

Middlewich! Intriguing town - heart and soul of county.
I told you not to cross it off. Enormous is its bounty.

Julie Elizabeth Smalley

BARROW-IN-FURNESS

Here in the place that's called Barrow
The Furness town that's got lots to show

Everyone friendly with a word of good cheer
You'll want to come back here year after year

Then building ships & submarines all the year round
The Navy can't do without Barrow on any ground

The Dock Museum's also here to tell
About Quayside for short walks as well

The town hall's good with clock face and chime to hear
But on the road right out of town the Furness Abbey is real
near

The place to visit where you must say yes
Has the name of Barrow-in-Furness

Julia Lawrence

HEAVEN IN THE LAKE DISTRICT

a little piece of heaven
away from the maddening crowd
a lovely carpet of bluebells
nestling between the lakeland hills

a bright sunny cloudless sky
a little robin passing by
the lapping at the water's edge
peace contentment a heartfelt sigh

between these hills and lakes of time
a rigorous capsulation
will be mine

a breath of clean fresh country air
quiet solitude for me is there
in this lakeland wonderland
my life's infinity to understand

Margery Rayson

MIDNIGHT IN MILLOM

The town is quiet
The park is empty
The clock strikes 12
MIDNIGHT IN MILLOM

The wind is whistling
The stars are bright
The moon is shining
MIDNIGHT IN MILLOM

The square is quiet
The street lamps shine on to the pavement
The houses are pitch dark
MIDNIGHT IN MILLOM

Craig Tyson

WATH BROW

Wath Brow is my Lakeland home
Were on the fells I loved to roam
Xmas trees in the woods
Trees enolving with new buds

Along the Ehen river we'd stray
Staying there to play all day
Decked along with trees so tall
Be sure in the beck, I would fall

When winter comes and I sit by the fire
The snowdrifts on fells are getting higher
There's nowhere I would rather be
At home on the Brow, with the family

Mary Taylor

THE FOUNDING FATHERS OF BARROW-IN-FURNESS

Schneider, Ramsden, Cavendish,
The roll call of history proclaims their names.
Two industrialists and a duke,
And the town that between them they made.

From fishing hamlet to crucible of industry,
A mere forty years flew by.
When street upon street of new brick houses sprung up,
Drawing multitudes hither by the magnet of wealth.

Some say the coming of the railway,
Gave birth to our town.
For it was laid side by side of a ruinous abbey,
Binding ancient and modern in vast enterprise.

I say the vital spark lay elsewhere,
That man's desire for riches was the hammer.
Whilst nature in all her bounty provided the anvil,
WIthout doubt Furness iron ore was Barrow's lodestar.

Fiona Lowe

THE DOLPHIN

Marra is a dolphin
That loves our Cumbrian coast
He could have chosen anywhere
But he favoured us the most
It was such a lovely sight
To see him swimming free
He fell in love with Maryport for everyone to see
He stayed within the harbour walls
And would not go away
Hundreds flock to see him there, every single day
They tried to chase him back to sea
But he just would not go
In the end they had to tow him free
It was the place for him to be
But now he has returned again along the Silloth coast
He swam right up the shore line
So beautiful to see
I'm pleased I've seen him once again
It filled my heart with glee

Brenda Wood

MEMORIES IN THE MIST

Roll in, roll in, you morning mist
to ride these waves, on swirling sea.
Rise past the lighthouse, long in darkness
into our harbours if you please.

Once these streets heard footsteps of slaves
chains that rattled on cobbled stone.
Then the coal rolled through the gates
through which the mining trade was born.

Tall ships linger there within you
sails a blowing in high winds caught.
Memories of a time gone by
welcome all to our Maryport.

Yvonne Wilson

CUMBRIA

Day breaks over the Borwich Rails and the birds have sung
awake,
The sheep have started standing in their oversize top coats.
The lights of the early risers come on in Millom Town,
And the stalagmite of Saint George's points to the lighten-
ing dawn,
And I walk where Norman walked and sit where he once
sat,
Where beneath my feet the men of iron once dug red
haematite.
The wild flowers lift their heads to worship the rising sun
And the sea holly prickles in the morning breeze and a new
day's begun.
The swaying margarettes remind me of you
And the sun turns the Duddon sands to gold.

Richard Robert Glennerster

A NEW DAY

Tomorrow is a new day
Especially for you.
You will not know what it contains
'Til the present day is through.
It may bring you joy and happiness,
Love you've never known,
Nice things which you dream about,
Yet have never been your own.
It could change a life completely
For the lonely and the sad.
In new friends who may touch your hearts
And leave them feeling glad.
Tomorrow is a new day,
Yet be mindful of today and of
The things that pleased you so.
We're part of yesterday for the
Past gave you each memory,
Held safe within your hearts
And they will always be a part of you
Each time a new day starts.

Sylvia Quayle

MILLOM TOWN'S WONDERFUL

Millom town's the place to be
If you want peace and tranquillity.
Lush green fields and a golden beach,
Lakeland fells within its reach.
Our heritage borne on iron ore,
Men's names steeped in folklore.
The relics of history
Our museum will keep
Where visitors call to take a peep.
Nostalgia there lies within
Showing the way that life has *bin.*
Walks are plentiful
Over hill and down dale,
Nothing but beauty to your avail.
Diversity helps this town to last
Enriched with the memory of its past.
Rugged are the local,
Friendly and vocal,
Upbeat, honest and true
Living together the way that they do.

Graham Lupton

SEASONS OF THE YEAR

In spring we see the daffodils
Dancing in the breeze
We sit upon the garden seat
At feel we're at our ease

When summer comes we plant the bedding
Which takes a bit of time
And when we see the birds arrive
We know that things are fine

In autumn when the leaves all fall
We know to take the rake
To tidy now we're just in time
A Christmas cake to bake

When winter comes we feed the birds
We get the usual flock
Of bluetits, robins and many more come without a fear
And then the frost and snow appear
We finally start another year

Grace Sloan

SUNDAY MORNINGS

Sleeping deep, down on my bed,
I'm there till half past ten.
Sleeping down, upon my bed,
Till oops! I'm late again.

I'm grumpy and gruff,
I'm big and I'm tough.
Not to mention my temper.
I storm into work,
Like an idiot jerk,
And the lads say
"There's no work today!"

Danika Lewis

MY HOME TOWN

Millom was once a bustling town
With a famous poet of renown
An ironworks thriving with trade
Hodbarrow mines for many a decade
The miners they were full of grit
Toiling hard down in the pit
Alas it's all gone but the folk have not
Well what have we now? What have we got?
We've Black Combe we can see for many a mile
Climb it you must, it's a test and a trial
The beautiful beaches, the golden sand
Take a leisurely stroll, walk hand in hand
The edge of the Lake District is where we live
With all of the beauty that it has to give
Where do you live? Millom you say
I'd like to visit it one fine day

Marjory Cocker

AN ODE TO THE RED MEN

A peninsular rich in Hematite ore
'Twas potential Britons and Romans both saw
They mined and smelted long before
Cistercian Monks extracted this mineral raw
Barrow-in-Furness, it may be said, exists because of this
mineral red
So from a hamlet, formally known as 'Barrie'
Sprang a port that ships may carry
Furness blood, mined from sop and vein
And from this blood red, there would be gain
With vision and forethought enough to inspire
A town spewed forth from men's desire
Red men mined whilst *furnace men* cast
The fruits of their labour destined to last
Bessemer Steel did become, from Barrow-in-Furness a
world number one
The rails that were rolled sent far and wide
Marked *Barrow Steel* and sent out with pride
The natural progression could only be
Constructing the finest vessels at sea
Liners, aircraft carriers, submarines too
From the sweat of many and the vision of few.

Vincent Hall

SUNSET OVER THE SOLWAY

The crimson orb of shimmering light
Slips slowly down the evening tide.
Its brightness caressing each rippling wave
In turn before cascading onto the sand.

A lone seagull soars above
Following the golden path
Across the water, then flying higher
In splendid isolation.

The scarlet globe, diminished now,
Falters in her majesty
And dark shadows creep in relentlessly
With dubious intent.

A chill steals in, as the sun's dying rays
Reach ever upwards to the sky.
The mountains in stark relief, sigh
And settle down to slumber, without a fight.

And the earth awaits
The dawn of another day
When the cycle
Will begin again.

Carolyn P Williamson

MY LITTLE TOWN

This town is a friendly little place
People leading lives at a sedate pace
They see no need to rush here and there
Conversations exist just about everywhere

This little town is without doubt the best
With panoramic views we have been blessed
In spring we hear new born lambs bleating
In the Civic Hall there's many a public meeting

This place has had its slice of glory
Hear about rum smuggling at the Rum Story
Various delicacies to give your tastebuds a treat
The flower arrangements in town cannot be beat

We've got the mountains, we've got the fells
We've got the early morning peals of church bells
We've got ancient ruins with many stones
Come and hear of the notorious John Paul Jones

We've got amenities where children can play
And we have shelter for the homeless to stay
So if at any time you are feeling down
Come join the happy throng in Whitehaven Town

Brian Brailey

OLD TOWN

I love this old town of Millom,
The place where I was born,
With its mountains, hills and sea,
Flowers, birds and bees,
And think to myself how lucky I have been.

Rita Brocklebank

CONISTON

They made heaven from a mountain.
They dug out the mountains secrets
and from them built a home;
they kept the darkness of the world away
and made a paradise of stone.

The mountains secrets are in the walls.
They live in the bones of the people
and whisper of a world long gone;
they tell of the people who went before
and of the places our souls are from.

Time stops here.
It takes a rest, builds a nest
out of goodness of people's deeds;
where a man can find his place here
he'd have everything he needs.

David Hilton

THE MUGGING

A bleak night and I hear footsteps of people chattering
Among themselves and flashing lights go by, blood is flow-
ing
From my mouth. My shirt is roughened, ripped and wrin-
kled, I lay
On this concrete ground unconscious with a beating heart
Perspiring brow and back and dizziness thinking,
remembering
I was drunk through the night, I was set on by a gang of
youths
Fists flying, pockets intruded, I was the mugging and no
one
Helped me!

Martin F Holmes

ALLONBY BAY

Sometimes the sea is calm and blue
The hills and fells a perfect view
Sometimes the sea is dark and grey
When I look out from Allonby Bay
Oyster catchers lift and fly
At the slightest sound as I go by
Like a ballerina the heron gracefully treads
Food is plenty on the mussel beds
The sea birds here don't seem to mind
As long as there is food to find
Diving in the stormy sea
They do deserve their fish for free
Terns come tumbling from the sky
I marvel at the speed they fly
Roaring waves and foaming crests
That's the sea that I like the best
The sea looks different every day
When I look out from Allonby Bay

Norah Twentyman

A MAGICAL PLACE

Sense magical change and rebirth
Parading daffodils ensuing mirth
Joyful song birds proudly call
From blossom trees in Ladyhall

Gaze forth across the bay
Welcoming glorious summer day
May my feet always fall
Upon the paths of Ladyhall

Admiring autumn's colourful dancing shimmer
Rustling leaves, fires glimmer
Gladdened spirits soar so tall
Within peaceful haven of Ladyhall

Know winters frost and bite
Days cold as night
Oh how I adore all
The velvet seasons of Ladyhall

Amanda Gaston

THE YOUTHS DOWN OUR WAY

Daunting to see them crowded like a pack treat them with
respect, they may respect you right back.

A handful do wrong causing all sorts of trouble, dare to
confront them you will get it back double.

The good, the bad and the damn right pretentious, day
after day their behaviour unnerves us.

You can't do much to change their ways, I'm afraid it's the
way things are these days.

Caron Rankin

HOME AWAY FROM HOME

A home is always away from home
And happiness a state of mind

We do not aspire for much
When everything is beyond reach

Life is set for a cause
Love is upset for a pause

Who can satisfy who?
And if so, for how long?

What is taken is to give back
What is not taken is to be left

After all, happiness is a state of mind
And our home is always away from home

Anantha Rudravajhala

CHEADLE VILLAGE

Cheadle Village is a nice little place and its little church of
St. Mary's is its unsung ace.
It's a must to be visited while you are here, afterwards pop
into the local and have a beer.
There's a good selection of shops in which to browse or
buy, and I'm sure you'll find something that'll catch your
eye.
The village green is a delight to the eye, so enjoy the flowers
and trees as you pass by.
Abney Hall is a curious place with an interesting history
and gardens of taste.
If you want to eat, there's plenty of places along the high
street, so stay for awhile and have some fun it's especially
nice when we get some sun.

Robert Laing

MILNROW'S POET GROUP

When using our local library,
As a place for us to meet;
To air our views on poetry,
Both written and spoken that week.
The group would meet collectively,
Each fortnight, on a Thursday,
Their poems, chosen selectively,
For each to read and have their say.
A different theme for every time,
Good poems we would write;
Using verse that would rhyme,
It is a way to express,
What is in our heart.
A gift of words, I guess,
That some of us impart.

Margaret Ridgway

IKEA HAS COME TO ASHTON

Ikea has come to Ashton, Ikea's my favourite store.
All my dreams rolled into one, right at my front door.
When first it was announced many folk were so dismayed,
But I watched with awe as the blue and yellow shape
became displayed.
Opening day's arrived at last, October 19th 2006, 10am is
here,
I'm stood waiting in the queue my shopping head put into
gear.
I love their many gadgets and furniture to build,
With my hammer, nails and drill I'm feeling pretty skilled.
Ikea's a huge four storey building, you simply cannot miss,
Right in the middle of Ashton town, a little bit of Swedish
bliss.
I'll visit Ikea every week come wind or rain or shine,
No more Warrington or Leeds, Ikea has come to Ashton-
under-Lyne.

Marguerite D Moss

THE TREE

Meandering fingers, grasping at clouds, reaching and
twisting up high,

Long slender arms, enveloping round, comforting, soothing
the sky,

Strong sturdy roots, burrowing down, twisting far into the
ground,

Standing rugged and hard, with unbreakable bark, passive,
inactive, no sound.

Sharp jagged buds, tearing at skin, punishing those who
dare climb,

Velvety leaves, on a whispering breeze, collecting the
seconds of time.

Julia Hagreen

BOLTON

Bolton folk, we are the salt of the earth.
Oh yes, great we are, what are we worth?
Loving and lively, caring and true.
Top of the league, well that's nothing new.
Open, helpful and above all proud.
Need a friend? Pop up north, join the crowd.
The statue of sport - their faces smile down.
On Bolton, Lancs, that great northern town.
We have soap stars and sports stars,
Big Sam and Amir.
You can ask them a question,
You know they are sincere.
What about Samuel Crompton
and his spinning mule,
And that Peter Kay, now there's a fool,
And as Fred Dibnah would say
with his little oily hat -
Did you like that?

J Burrows

BURY TOWN CENTRE

Come with a smile, not a frown
to Bury's famous market town,
Like to shop, till you drop
with lots of bags, you'll want to stop.

So put them down and rest your feet,
In one of our cafés, have something to eat.
Bury's black pudding with mustard - Yum
You're sure to find something to fill your tum.

In the Mill Gate there's lots to choose
Your child is safe, you will not lose.
Put them in a taxi or police car
Push them around and you'll go far.

Oh my gosh, how fast it's flown
I've ran out of dosh,
So it's time to go home.

Michelle Heatley

SEA OF FACES

Multicoloured city vibrant and alive
A plethora of passion once destroyed
Nature springs its finery deep within your soul
Conversations assault their struggle to be heard
How I miss you when I travel
Ever yearning to return to bask in your warmth
Silently I sit secure, safe
Today you stand tall and proud
Each gleaming window shows its wares
Refusing to die as once its centre shattered

My pride knows no boundaries
You draw me into gentle caring hands

Homeless people smile in greeting
Oasis of calm in psychedelic madness
My home town
Exploded, exposed, ever evolving

Lynn Noone

MY AUTUMN GARDEN

The cool winds are blowing, dusk is near, one
solitary gladiola stays aloof, the roses long
since gone, and the grass no longer a pertinent
green. Horse chestnuts lie mockingly around the
lawns, the fallen leaves show off their autmn
gold as they swirl around the paths. The sycamore
seeds hover slowly to the ground amongst the
multitude of *crystals* making up their winter's
cocoon in preparation for the myriad of colour
in the spring to follow, as ever leaving us
speechless. How cruel that we poor mortals
are left by nature, to come out next spring,
Looking one year older.

Mark Goode

BURY LIFE

Life in Bury is all I know
I've seen it develop and grow
People come from all around
Just to visit our famous town

Market days three times a week
Family and friends gather to meet
Loaded up with bargains galore
Still lots more time to explore

Museum arts and crafts
Bury history from the past
Steam train rides for all ages
Carries you away to different places

Rose Glover

DUCK

Skidaddle and squabble, waddle puddled flats,
skating shines, and mobbing on torn off crusts.
Bottles of mallard green chortle and burst
out, dismantling on their Liverbird wings.

Geese stretch and peck on sneaky Nessie necks,
while grebes crest, and dive for sparks in the murk.
Bread squeaks on boozers plates, and a wasp jerks
insane between twinned and kissing beakers.

An afternoon merges suburbia
with something resembling life, and time limps
under May. Offspring spoil themselves and jump,
when the wasp sings, and stings free and early

as bees should. Water skiers buzz past,
and scatter tsunamis across the glaze.
The lake cracks. The flocks explode in throttles.
A syringe squeezes in the margins, offering peace.

Owen Lowery

ROCHDALE

Cobbled streets,
Old buildings,
Church,
High rise flats,
Town centre,
Co-op,
Touchstones art gallery,
Empty buildings,
Town hall,
Shop windows,
Big issue sellers,
Market,
Sweet stalls,
Charity shops,
Pubs,
People

This is my town
Is it like yours?

Katherine Helen Wroe

REVISITING PLACES

Revisiting places we once thought we knew,
Most now demolished, replaced with brand new.

Small terraced houses, two up and two down,
Back to back dwellings made up our small town.
Old cobbled streets where we played our team games,
Brick walls gouged out or all sprayed with rude names.
Corners we met and our gangs hung around,
We've never forgotten our childhood playground.

Everything shared from our rooms to our baths,
Halving our troubles with sweet tea and laughs.
Cold, outside toilets in the dark, silent yards,
Front doors were unlocked, back entries unbarred.
Warmth from our siblings we sought in our beds,
Though often unwashed we were always well fed.

Revisiting places we once thought we knew,
Old buildings have vanished, fond memories stay true.

Barbara Peachey

CRINGLE PARK

In Levenshulme there's a place called Cringle Park.
Where I've chatted to friends on logs.
Although I'm grown up the joy it brings,
swinging high upon the swings.
The stream trickles through the banks.
And in the summer and spring,
The flowers much colour they bring.
Dandelions, daisies and daffodils.
Lots of pretty bushes.
Once I hugged a tree there.
Sitting on the benches in the sun.
This park is such fun.

Rachel Van Den Bergen

IF ONLY

There's cobwebs on my heart strings,
It seldom gets used today.
The girls have all got married,
And gone their seperate ways.
I sit and sometimes wonder,
Just what might have been.
But now upon this bottom shelf,
I only have my dreams.
I still can hear the laughter,
As we danced into the night.
Sometimes into the morning,
As the dawn was shining bright.
I feel the lace of their embrace,
Their kisses on my lips.
There in my mind, all the time,
As on this shelf I sit.

Alan Withers

BOWL TOWN

Bowl Town as named long ago,
Encircled by hills, in winter covered with snow,
Our town in the bowl gives a welcome to all.
For those that may stay or just pay a call.

A bowl of riches worth more than gold.
A city in waiting for all it's fold
To be born and grow to live and learn.
To remain in its splendour is what we yearn.

In the past are the memories of times gone by
When red brick towers reached for the sky.
The acrid pollution of industrial fogs
The hustle and bustle of clattering clogs.

Its people , its soul radiate its worth.
Its warmth, its magic no better on earth.
A few moments of time and your heart will be won,
Because the grass is no greener than in Bolton.

Arnold Harrison

LONGFIELD 1950's

Longfield is a long straight street
With shops and houses all very neat
If you walk right to the top
You'll see the station where the train will stop
Barbara Taylors is the shop that sells beer
My Dad likes this shop
Why is not clear
Alfreds the toffee shop with jars in a row
He says hurry up and don't be slow
Then there's the post office you can go use the phone
I wonder what it's like, we don't have one at home
Chemist on the corner with men in white coats
Mixing all kinds of medicine for coughs and sore throats
Also two chippies both very good
You get fish and chips or steak and kidney pud.
Dorothy Buntings I've saved to the last
It makes your mouth water just walking past
On a tray in the window all lined up nice
Is the worlds very best vanilla slice

Heather Kaye

A SONNET FOR NORMA

I go out for my exercise most days whether sun or rain
Just as we often used to do before that fateful day
When God took your hand and led you to his garden to
remain
And left me sad and lonely without you far away.

As I walk the meadow I know you're by my side
We loved the scent of new mown grass, the fragrant
elderflower
The sight of little rabbits or squirrels hopping off to hide
The birdsong from the trees as the church bell tolls the
hour.

We were never lonely, we had our love to share
Now I must soldier on alone with sorrow in my soul
But knowing that deep in my mind I still have you to care
To help me through these final years until I reach my goal.

Before too long I'll get the call in God's own special way
Once more we'll be together, forever and a day.

Ken Bradbury Harrop

THE JOYS OF DANCING

Dear Walter for this poem so good,
My deepest thanks I hand you.
Although I dance like a log of wood,
You're a brick, how did I land you?

You never moan or groan
When I step on your toes.
You take it with a great big smile,
And then turn up your nose.

When Ena and her husband endeavour,
To teach me the cha cha
They may as well give up forever,
It's all a lot of ha ha.

Next time we're out upon the floor
Just swing me round your head,
Right through the bandstand,
Through the door,
And will my face be red.

Joyce Torkington

HEYWOOD

A couple in love forever
A suicide bridge
A park filled with laughter
Dog walkers near
Shops in the centre
Market up the road
Schools not so far
Pubs galore
A *Crusty the Clown*
Round the corner
A loving Grandma
Up the street
Youths out boozin'
Civic shows for all to see
This is our town
Simple as can be
It's the place
Where I grew
Into the woman
I might be

Katie Haigh

WELCOME VISITOR

A guided tour of Bolton could open wide your eyes.
The town hall and the precinct - would be a real surprise.
The crescent with its arches, adjoining buildings too,
Architectural grandeur stands proud for all to view.

Multi-stores and retail shops with bargains by the score,
Abundant choice for everyone and fashion shops galore.
Restaurants for high class meals and cafes for a nibble,
Menus vary with their fayre, at prices one can't quibble.

There are health clubs, night clubs and clubs of every kind.
Theatres, cinemas, libraries - for those with active minds.
Interesting country parks - to stroll or congregate.
Churches for the reverent - to kneel and meditate.

Smithills Hall and Halli'th' Wood are places not to miss.
Barrow Bridge and Last Drop village - bound to bring pure
bliss.
Travel to the outskirts and see the countryside,
Rivington, West Pennine Moors - all part of Bolton's pride.

Kathleen Frances West

MY DAD

My Dad loves chocolate and coffee,
Along with delicious, soft toffee.
He eats it like there's no tomorrow,
But when we run out, he sits and cries in sorrow!

My Dad fixes engines and JCB's,
He has very bony knees.
He loves to go and watch Bury FC,
He's the best Dad in the world to my sister and me!

Jennifer Starkie

KNOWL HILL

At the top of our lane is a view so rare,
of Knowl Hill and the moors, of which I care,
So special the sight on a sunny day,
The clouds making pattern along the way,
Just to think what windfarms could do to this view,
makes one despair, even if only a few
were allowed to be on such a hill,
To take away our pleasure against our will,
We are so lucky to have this fine sight,
On our doorstep, it appears in the light
of the morning so proud with an air of mystery,
Looking down on our town and all its history,
We hope and we pray the powers that be,
Listen to opinions of the people they see,
Take into consideration what will be lost,
By allowing these windmills and at what cost!

Doris Turner

BOLTON TOWN

Gone are the clogs and bonnets and shawl.
Gone is the spinning wheel and joiners awl.
The cotton mills now banished from the Bolton scene
There's hardly a trace of where they've been
But like a phoenix rising from their past,
The market place in splendour cast.
Welcoming people to come and share
Bolton's new skyline depicted there.
Bolton town in history steeped
The Earl of Derby his head could not keep.
If the Jacobites returned to Bolton again,
Would they recognise their old domain?
Our coat of arms bears an elephant crest
And an elephant trail is there to test.
Civic centre of architectural beauty
Guarded by lions doing their duty.
Pulsating nightlife, vibrant venues,
Colourful scene, enticing menus.
Ongoing transition from old to new
Bolton, I'll always remember you.

Kathleen Hinks

RADCLIFFE

As I stand here on Radcliffe Bridge,
Looking down on Irwell's stream
My thoughts turn to my old town
And I begin to dream.
I dream about the old tower
De Radcliffe family seat.
The medieval manor
Where Roch and Irwell meet.
The church and the old tower
Have both been handed down
From Radcliffe down to Sussex
The jewels in the crown,
I dream of the industrial age
When Radcliffe reigned supreme,
With cotton, mines and railways
They're all there in my dream.
Engineering, we were grand
Paper? We just ruled the land.
Bleaching, dyeing, and much more
The canal? It came to our front door!

John T Boardman

MAMA'S SALUTATION

Ma' Mama', what a woman,
Her life, her history,
From Africa, ta' the Middle-East, ta' South Asia an' ta' here
in the UK
That's ma' Mama', she a Queen,
She raised me you see,
She was both Mami an' Daddy,
She sho' did God proud, look how I turned out,
I'm so gracious, yet I could never ever repay her,
Not in this lifetime, never,
You see, ma' Mama',
She a display of a woman,
A woman where man come from,
Unless you talking 'bout Eve comin' outta' Adam's left rib,
But anyway,
Usually, a man will love, honour an' obey his Mama',
These days it seems he can't do the same for his wife, his
woman,
You ever thought 'bout that?
They say a man will choose a woman, jus' like his Mama',
In ma' case that's very apparent, no front, no drama,
Ma' woman, is jus' like ma' Mama'.

Billal Mahmood

OLDHAM'S MARK OWEN TAKE THAT SUPERSTAR

The logo emblazoned with the double T logo
Posters on your sister's bedroom, the five dolls
Perfume and memorabilia
Nineteen ninety two, the year of Take That
And an Oldham lad called Mark Owen
From Oldham five guys with a dream
They came, saw and conquered
The U.K charts but in ninety-six, five became four
And shortly after they split up fans cried
For days and days after
The shock announcement
Mark Owen lives in Lake Windermere
And a father he is now
A come back and single in two thousand and six for Take
That.

Sean Harewood

Born in Oldham, **Sean Harewood** started writing poetry to
express his inner thoughts. "My work is influenced by my
inner-self and my self-conscious state and I would like to
be remembered as a different kind of poet," he pointed out.
Aged 38, Sean works for Oldham Council and has
ambitions to be a multi-millionaire and superstar DJ. "The
people I would most like to meet are Michael Jackson, R
Kelly and The Rocksteady Crew. "If I could be anyone for
the day it would be David Beckham, P Diddy or Jay Z,"
said Sean. "My biggest fantasy is two women in a hot tub
and my biggest nightmare is not to find true love."

LOCAL POEM

Jerusalem

I shall not cease from mental fight,
Nor shall my sword sleep in my hand,
Till we have built Jerusalem
In England's green and pleasant land

St. Luke's Church, historic spire,
centrefold of a miller's town
grown old in ways of industry.
Stone placed by history's hands
on stone placed by hands before,
when all this was fielded,
when hands before had fetched the granite.
They were, no doubt,
christened here, married here, buried here:
those who placed
the final blocks,
and wound the clock that took their time.

I sit beneath a sycamore,
and listen to their hymn.

Samuel Fisher

PORTALS OF PEACE

Lancashire life as history reveals, Bury's mills acting as
centralised wheels.
Generations worked hard and long, enlivening the day with
cheerful song.

Looking to the future diminishing fears, alleviating some
working class tears.
Post-war Britain arrived on the scene, including housing
improvements with patches of green.
Functional designs offering an easier life, and relieving the
tensions of marital strife.
A return to gardening was lovely to see, personally
landscaped artistically.

Pioneering businessmen in Bury were born, rebuilding the
town for the lost and forlorn.
War-weary and beginning again, heroes normality was hard
to attain.
Parks, libraries, architecture and art, mindful duties for the
rich to impart.
Divinely created by people inspired, to uplift all the
residents overly tired.

Sylvia Lee

BURRS COUNTRY PARK

Burrs Country Park is the place to be
Lots of birds to feed and to see
There's an old tower, part of a mill
And in the distance is Holcombe Hill
Ducks, geese and swans floating around
Quacking and hissing and making some sound
So Burrs Country Park is the place to be
A beautiful place which is wild and free

Graham Scotson

PANTO TIME

Panto time is happy I've always said,
Happy memories flood in my head.
Queuing around the theatre *Grand*
Mi 'and tucked pleasantly in my mam's 'and
An orange fert' interval in mi pocket,
Whilst eatin' a warm pastie, yet couldn't knock it.
Once we sat reet up int gods -
Cheapest seats, but it made no odds,
The theatre *Grand* was packed t'ert ceilin',
The antics of Frank Randal sent us reelin',
Joseph Locke was there wi' a song
We all joined in, it din't tek us long.
There was Hylda Baker, ee, what a trooper,
One of my favourites, I thought she was super.
Why did they destroy the dear old *Grand*
Where I queued wi mi 'and in my dear mam's 'and.

Louise Gillard

WHAT YOU WILL FIND IN BURY

Bury is a market town, it's steeped in history.
The birthplace of Sir Robert Peel,
A pleasant place to be.
I like the modern shopping mall,
And surrounding countryside.
Coaches bring in visitors,
From places far and wide,
To visit our famous market, and have a look around,
And where, on any market day, a bargain may be found.
Black puddings are their speciality, for these they are
renowned,
And even strangers sample them, when they come to town.
Though many things remain the same,
There have been changes too,
And we have the traditional, alongside the new,
The people here are friendly folk.
They will have a laugh, and share a joke.
So if you have never visited this northern market town,
You will find a treat awaits you, come and have a look
around.
There are many lovely things to see, so don't be in a hurry,
And enjoy the hospitality, that you will find in Bury.

Irene McWilliam

PRESTWICH VILLAGE

Once a quiet priest's retreat
Where sheep were ushered down a village lane,
Now is heard the continuous roar of traffic
On its daily journey to and from Manchester.

A city once with a sooty veil of grime and poverty
That gave birth to the Industrial Revolution.
Yet in Preswich cloughs with ancient horse pack trail
Always children have laughed and played by the bubbling
brook.

In Prestwich Village botanists once gathered
To study the rare flowers these cloughs proudly displayed.
On a hill the bells of Saint Mary's church still chime
A witness to life's cycle and the passing of time.

This village church is also a stage
Where Coronation Street actors play their part,
The trials and tribulations of the local TV soap.
Meanwhile in the village cafés the genteel ladies meet for
lunch
And for a moment time moves slower by in Prestwich
Village.

Lilian Lines

AN OLD MARKET TOWN

First we address an old market town
A sixteenth century history and a Pennine surround
A tale of a *Black Knight* some ghosts here and there
Canals, parks and rivers and an annual fair
A writer well known in a *Tipperary Song*
With a heart felt welcome, how can you go wrong
Take in all of the sites, some mentioned above
And what was once a small *hamlet* is our town full of love

Carol-Anne Wheelton

ROCHDALE, MY HOME TOWN

Me knee high I look to the sky, smoky mills and rolling
hills,
Gracie Fields and charity shields.

A winding canal not used anymore, some say now just an
eyesore.

Sparking clogs and barking dogs, lots of cobbles and push-
bikes wobble.
Chills and ills, coughs, no pills.

It's always raining and the sky's so grey, peoples faces
reflect dismay.
A knocker up wanders around oh what a sound, the smell
of bread, wish we could stay in bed.

Rochdale my home town.

Janice Cheetham

UP THE DALE

When it's freezing and lashing with rain
Can we bear to put up with the pain
Are we masochists all
Obsessed with football
We few who have turned out again?

We're fighters through thick and through thin
There's no towel that we're throwing in
We'll urge on the blues
Come win, draw or lose
But how long until our next win?

The class on the pitch may be lacking
And our manager due for a sacking
But no other club
Outdoes us for grub
Our pies at half-time are just cracking.

Did I see some silverware gleam?
The cup held aloft by my team
Have we joined the few
And just beat Man U?
Well no - but at least we can dream.

Ian Aitchison

GRANDCHILDREN AND GREAT GRANDCHILDREN

We love their smiling faces
Skin that is smooth and clear
Little legs running all around
Just makes us want to cheer

Little legs running everywhere
Shouting come and see
Little arms waving in the air
Shouting look at me

They run behind the sofa
Shouting peek a boo
Chuckling with joy
When we peek a boo them too

They are so small and oh so sweet
Creeping round on tiny feet
What can we their grandparents say
Except that we love them more each day

Then at night with little faces all aglow
We give them a hug saying off to bed you go
Soon fast asleep and oh so small
Little angels are God's greatest gifts of all

Jean Flatters

MY TOWN

I live just a bus ride from Salford.
The town where Lowry did his thing.
I bet if he painted on a Saturday afternoon
he could have heard the Chaddy end sing,
singing a song with heart and soul
to spur on our town teams side.
Just up the road from our famous hospital
where Doctor Steptoe worked with pride.
It's only a stones throw to the civic centre
that cast shadows on our busy shopping town.
To some locals it could never be the same
since our old market hall burnt down.
I would love to ride in a hot air balloon,
not so high that I couldn't look down
to the cobbled streets and chimney tops.
To my home in Oldham Town.

Denise Wild

Born in Oldham, **Denise Wild** started writing poetry after a
visit to her grandmothers graveside. "I was searching for
memories and was inspired to write poetry," she explained.
"My work is influenced by family, friends and workmates
and I would describe my style as coming from the heart. I
would like to be remembered with a smile." Aged 45,
Denise works as a bakery operative and has an ambition to
live long enough to see how *Coronation Street* ends. She
has a partner, Julia and would most like to meet Jane
MacDonald the singer and presenter. "I have a book *Wild
about Life* being published at the moment and I have writ-
ten about 300 poems," added Denise.

PROGRESS IN REVERSE

I've lived in our village many long years,
Sometimes with happiness, sometimes tears,
But the village I knew long ago,
Has changed much since it started to grow.

Gone the green fields surrounding the place,
Builders came and took all the space,
Now there are office blocks of concrete and glass,
A motorway and an underpass.

On the edge of the village new houses were built
For people from the city who had no guilt,
When fields and hedges where wild flowers grew,
Now sprout tin cans and plastic of every hue.

Now aeroplanes to and from the airport roar overhead,
Make enough noise to awaken the dead.
The village at night was quiet and serene,
Now rowdy teenagers shout and scream.

Old faces and neighbours they've drifted away,
Not many left from yesterday.
Tried fighting planners, no chance of winning,
I wish it was all back as in the beginning.

Margaret Fox

THE CASTLEFIELD CANAL BASIN

My poem is about Castlefield,
Where two canals which meet,
The Bridgewater and the Rochdale,
Near Coronation Street.

In the early years of waterways,
Horses towed the barge,
A means of transportation,
With cargoes small and large.

Canals became neglected,
Work had to be done,
With programmes of restoration,
Hence areas for relaxation and fun.

An inn called *Dukes* for refreshments,
Stands near Castlefield Lock,
A frontage with tables and benches,
In summer people will flock.

The Castlefield Hotel and YMCA
To me an appealing sight,
Overlooking the jetty where boats are moored,
With narrow boats all spotless and bright.

Frank Warren

BEST OF BOLTON

Bolton is a great place to live
it just has so much to give
There's Walter Hall and the town hall clock
just standing there tick, tock
If you are lost and on your own
there are lots of people to make a home
There are lots of things to keep you active
and also keep your brain factive
Bolton is controlled and on the run and lots
of things to make it fun
So please consider it a place to live because we have so
much to give

Taylor Coppell

SPRINGFIELD, WIGAN

I am a lady of middle age, small, petite,
I am in this area the whole seven days of the week.
My job, school welfare, I am there for that too,
A suit isn't needed, nor a high heeled shoe.
An overall, whistle, pad and some pens,
Gets me through, 'til me hour and a half ends.
Child-minding I do after being in school. It takes me 'til
five,
I take them for a swim, walks in park, or a ride.
Saturdays do fairs, car boot sales,
Sundays it's church, receiving God's blessing at
communion rails.
This is what I think keeps me young, alive,
I rate it better than a job, nine through 'til five.
I meet lots of people, see new sites,
Have no need for tablets, fast asleep with telly and dimmed
lights.

Doreen Baggaley

BURY

Bury isn't my birthplace,
Though choice didn't enter that sphere,
I came to live here through marriage,
And I'm oh so glad I am here.

How do I begin to describe it?
The warmth that comes from within,
There's so much to do here in Bury,
I don't know where to begin.

The market engulfs me with colours,
The choice oh where do I start?
And don't forget our black puddings,
Worldwide taste that sets them apart.

The mill gate, the rock and the plaza,
Shops that fulfil every whim,
Restaurants, cafes and snack bars,
Even baths if I fancy a swim.

If it's culture I want it surrounds me,
The town hall fusiliers, Robert Peel,
I love this town in its glory,
This town so full of appeal.

Sandra Jones

BORN IN BURY

I'm a Bury lad me,
Bury born and bred,
I was born in Fairfield Hospital,
Bury Cemetery when I'm dead.

It's famous for its puddings,
Chadwicks make them black,
We've got a famous market,
People are always coming back.

Our football team's *The Shakers*,
They really shake them up,
We still hold the record,
For the score in the FA Cup.

We have some famous people;
Peter Skellen, Victoria Wood,
The founder of the police force,
The Wylde is where he's stood.

Bury folk take nowt for granted,
They are never sad or down,
So if you want to meet nice people,
Come down to Bury Town.

Ian Stone

HOLLINGWORTH LAKE

Hollingworth Lake, it seemed so far,
Especially as we had no car.
A family outing, that's mum, dad, sister and me,
A bus ride, a picnic, oh what would we see?
That huge span of water with boats bobbing up and down,
Just a bus ride away from our busy little town.
A pleasant walk all around, looking at houses so *posh,*
We knew if you lived there you had plenty of dosh.
Halfway round was a picnic break, it's what we had,
A running stream, oh a paddle along with our dad.
Oh we had an adventure, we saw fields with cows, horses and sheep,
Played games, laughed loads, hopped, skipped, walked, ran and did leap.
On the bus ride home, it seemed we had travelled such a long way,
Especially when tired out after such fun, happy, exhausted at the end of a brill day.
Childhood memories, I have such a lot,
Some I remember, how I could not!

Linda Flynn

Dedicated to my parents who made my childhood a memorable, pleasurable, thought-provoking and inspirational time in my life.

THE SHOPS

At Guide Bridge every shop you could mention,
Until the supermarket came - that wonderful invention.
Progress they call it, and I suppose I agree,
I so dearly loved those shops you see.

Shops that sold dresses, hats from next door,
Frothy concoctions who could ask for more.
If a headache should come your way,
Pill from the chemist, to keep it at bay.

Passing the greengrocers, fruit laid in rows,
Brightly coloured flowers tied up with bows.
Pot or a pan, or even a screw,
Hardware shop was there for you.

Need of a haircut, sir? No problem at all,
Gents outfitters would kit you out fit for a ball.
Bank and a newsagents for the latest news.
Post office that we thought we'd never lose.

Guide Bridge Station. catch a train near or far,
If you were thirsty there was even a bar.
With great sadness I mourn their decline,
I'm off to the computer to shop online.

Eve Ingham

A LEGEND

I saw a man in Bolton
Wandering around the town
He was a Bolton Wanderer
A man of some renown

He hadn't *kicked the bucket*
As some folk had thought
He was standing on the corner
Just by St Andrew's court

When asked for his autograph
He signed it straight away
No bother at all, he said
You can ask me any day

The little lad with his pen and book
Well, purred just like a cat
And ran back to his mam
And she said, well done Nat

Yes it was Nathaniel Lofthouse
A legend to behold
I recall yelling many times
It's a goal! It's a goal! It's a goal!

Eric Tomlinson

MY HOMETOWN BURY

I'd like to talk of Bury
That special place I live,
Our Art Gallery and Library
Much knowledge have to give.

We know Gibraltar has a rock
Well we possess one too,
It is a street just full of shops
With lots of things to do.

And don't forget our Steam Train
It's super and quite swell,
It travels right through Summerseat
And Ramsbottom as well.

We have a famous market
The finest in the land,
People come from far and wide
To behold this sight so grand.

Do you wonder why I love it
And never wish to roam?
My roots are well embedded
In this place which I call home.

Eva Smith

MANCHESTER, DEAR MANCHESTER

In days of yore you were known for your cotton,
And memories of that will ne'er be forgotten,
But the city, today, is a magical place -
It has a new and unforgettable face!

So come soon and visit some old parts of town -
There's The Shambles and old Hanging Ditch.
And perhaps see the Corn Exchange - now called The Triangle,
Where the shops are exotic and the décor quite rich.

Castlefield, too, is a part to explore,
With its canals and cafés galore.
A place to escape from the hustle and bustle,
Have lunch and a drink - and much more!

The Commonwealth Games are just a memory now,
But the feeling of sport lingers on.
Manchester's name is still to the fore
And the spirit is second to none.

So, keep up the good work, Mancunians,
Look forward to vistas so clear.
There's so much talent amongst you,
You really have nothing to fear!

Shirley C Daniels

A TRUE TASTE OF LIFE IN RADCLIFFE

Roll up roll up, you too can live in Radcliffe town
All it takes is a deposit down

We've got flats, flats, and more flats being built
They won't stop building until we're full to the hilt

Just a word of warning though
Once you have parted with your dough

Because even when the roadworks are done
You will find it won't be very much fun

You will be stuck like the rest of us
Whether you're in a car, van or public bus

This town is always one massive traffic jam
And no one in authority gives a damn

Even if you decide to walk
The decline of the town will make you baulk

Still us diehards live in hope
We don't all just sit and mope

We've lobbied the council to improve our town
Let's hope it happens before the flats fall down

June Plaskett

BURY

Situated near the Pennine Hills,
Is Bury with its heritage of industrial mills.

Tall chimneys have gone, from the skyline disappeared,
The smoke has dispersed, the air has now cleared.

Bury has again won the prestigious crown,
For Britain in Bloom, voted the *Best Town*.

Its son Robert Peel, is famous of course.
He was responsible for the country's police force.

Based at Wellington Barracks, were the Lancashire
fusiliers,
Winning many honours during wartime years.

For intertown travel, Metrolink is supreme,
The restored East Lancs railway is regularly in steam.

To Bury's famous market, people come flooding,
Especially to sample its famous black pudding!

Bury's football team has been struggling, the fans expect
far more,
But the club still holds the proud record, the *Cup Finals
highest score*.

The town's future is bright, more able to compete,
When the new rock development is finally complete.

Derek Pepperdine

J McMULLEN, FAMILY BUTCHER

In war-torn London, Gwendolyn (with a y not i) born and
bred
Met bomb-disposal Joe and so were wed
She had to move North where his family belonged
Extended members departing, two daughters came along
The hereditary business now belonged to Joe
And Gwen delivered meat, to and fro
It settled her into Lancaster life
Delivery-lady, confidante, mother and wife
But in later years life dealt a blow
Their happy plan of retirement gone, Gwen a widow
After years of support Gwen was left to mourn
Joe, beloved husband's death, leaving her forlorn
So now Gwen meets friends at church, enjoying
after-service coffee
Visiting favourite charity shops in *Bluebell* her lifeline Mini.

Shirley Pinnington

LONGRIDGE

My home town was small,
People would call, everyone knew all.
Mum has lived in the same home for 50 year,
And she still lives here.
She and we delivered papers all over the place;
Up Berry, down Kestor, along Lower Lanes we'd race.

Now our town's bigger, old and new combined,
Still the old streets and new being built all the time.
More and more people and traffic too,
But still the same lovely people welcoming you.

So, if you come to Longridge, call at the Stonebridge.
It's quaint and part of our heritage.
There's an off-license, bed shop, café and TVs,
A chippy and Old Mill where my play centre's going to be.
There's a garage for fuel and our house on the block;
If you're in need of a cuppa, give us a knock.

Teresa Gethings

MOSNEY WOOD

The sun shines through the trees it's seen
The leaves become a dappled green.
The ground now covered in leaf mould
Protects new life as it unfolds.

The bluebells wave their sculptured heads,
The heavy scent it can be said
Flows through unhindered the woodland glade,
This beautiful place that God has made.

The deer are free to wander around
The fox and her cubs in their den underground.
The badger too frequents this place,
The rabbits, skittish, each other do chase.

The outside world though is closing in,
The green fields have gone, it's such a sin.
The paths newly made are now covered in mud,
The name of this place is Mosney Wood.

Patricia Bamber

A GRAND PLACE TO BE

Where can you go for laughter
Guaranteed fun and mirth
Where can you see a disaster
Or witness a death or a birth

Where can you sing and be happy
Or cry with a smile or a moan
Where can you go all by yourself
But know that you won't be alone

Where can you see all the glory
Of something restored to its best
The Grand Theatre of course is the answer
It rises above all the rest

The royal seal of approval is well deserved
It caters for young and for old
May it always supply us with pleasure
It's a place worth its whole weight in gold

                                        Susan Lord

LYTHAM WINDMILL

A windmill stands on Lytham Green
A landmark of the Fylde
Eighteen-o-five is when it was built
So it's been there quite awhile

Maybe it's sails no longer turn
And its function is no more
But still the people come to see
Such is its allure

And now instead of milling flour
A museum it's become
With memories of bygone days
Showing how then, things were done

Not as grand some may think
As its neighbour, Blackpool tower
But nevertheless majestic
A symbol of its power

Carole Lawrence

BLACKPOOL TOWER

Five hundred plus feet, of *Victorian* iron and steel,
Two years, six months of blood, sweat and zeal!
Evoking memories of childhood, we just cannot hide,
It's such an *Eiffel!* Beheld with artistic pride,

Peer out to sea, atop renowned edifice so high!
You'll beach shore you could almost touch the sky,
Take the *Walk of Faith,* gripped by penitent fear,
Pray *solemnly,* You're able to come back next year.

Ian Clayton

Born in Macclesfield in Cheshire, **Ian Clayton** has interests
including competitions, writing and keep-fit. "My work is
influenced by sincere people and my life experiences and I
would describe my style as deep, sincere, yet adaptable," he
pointed out. "I would like to be remembered for my discern-
ing nature and non-judgmental attitude." Aged 45, Ian is
an assistant manager with ambitions to succeed in his job,
better his living standards and travel the world. "I have
written short stories and personal verses and my biggest
fantasy is getting married underwater and I would also love
to own my own personal cinema," added Ian.

BURNLEY

Burnley is my birthplace
Burnley is my home
But Burnley's changed over the years
Which brings me very close to tears.

I love the town and the Lancashire folk
Our neighbours are like family
Always there to share a joke
Tea and sympathy on tap readily.

People have lived in the same house for many years
Take pride in their homes and are of good cheer
Everyone knows everyone else in the street
The community spirit is hard to beat.

The feeling of belonging
Is in the distant past
Now Burnley is multi cultural
And going European fast.

Barbara Hartley

LOOKING BACK, NOW FORWARD

There were two with long protruding decks
Reaching out to the brine so far,
The first being ruined by gales and the sea,
But the second was burned without hope.

Its skeleton was washed by the approaching tide,
An antiquity lost but not forgotten,
For these places are left empty and quiet,
But the earlier times proved their worth.

A big white hotel being brought back to life
For the years of desolation did take its toll,
Along with a theatre sharing the same fate,
There doors are looked forward to opening once again.

A good attraction that is loved by many
Stands on the promenade in preferred pose,
With steps up and replicas of birds to please,
For this is the setting where Eric Morecambe stands.

Stephen John Davidson

BET YOU WILL

Where do you live, Lancaster? Yes I said it's grand.
We've everything you can think of, even a brass band.
Go to the park at the top of yon hill
Lord Ashton's memorial is standing there still.
There's also a castle where murderers and witches were
hung
Mam told me the bogeyman lived there, when I was very
young.
Museum, library, Judge's Lodgings too
So much to see, so much to do.
Down at the Quayside in yesteryear
Many a merchant sailed his goods out of here.
A walk along the silver Lune, its wonders to behold
Listen to the fishermen, oh what stories they'd unfold.
The music room is tucked away in a quiet little square
It's very peaceful there.
So next time you're passing stop off if you will.
There's a lot lot more to Lancaster
You'll like it. *Bet you will.*

Pam Dixon

A LOST TOWN

Who pulled the market clock tower down,
and broke the hearts of Blackburn town,
then went mad, with pick and spade,
to do the same to Thwaites arcade.
Younger burgher's could not have known
the beauty that those shops had shown,
with tiled facades that shone like silk,
or the crying, when they'd spilled the milk,
the perpetrators, long since departed,
continued then at what they'd started.
So the demolition carried on,
how we miss what's long since gone.

Bill Austin

GALGATE - GATEWAY TO THE GALLOWS

Rhubarb city, the farmer's life
Till the land, sharpen the knife
Gateway to the gallows
The murderer's rest
For his penance pray
Drink to his rest.
The condemned man dreams
Of the surrounding streams
As the farmer's weary toil
Strives on bloodstained soil

So quietly sleep, Galgate's child
Live your daydream, so slow yet wild
Remember this life is only a loan
Death once remembered in this village, your home.

Dean Wakefield

ORMSKIRK

This pretty little West Lancs town
Where busy market traders ply
Their wares from stalls lined up and down
The narrow streets to passers by

Has at its centre cross a clock,
That facing four ways standing bold
Marks tick by tick, and tock by tock,
Where gingerbread was made of old,

The church has tower and steeple found
Stood side by side upon the ground.
The people here are warm and kind
As any others you may find.

You're welcomed here by kindly folk
Who love to smile and laugh and joke,
For people are most truly blessed
Who live in Ormskirk, Lancs South West.

Cecil E Beach

OUR VILLAGE

With marsh to the North, moss land to the South
Where grasses dance in obeyance of the winters cool breeze
Summer brings the aroma of new mown hay
It fills your nostrils and heightens the senses

We have our fair share of characters
Individuals who don't feel the need to be sheep
And follow the crowd

There's Auntie Ellie at the grand old age of 90
Played the organ four whole hours to help build a school
In Uganda, now she's gained an MBE now really what
could be grander

Friendly faces greet you at our local shop
When it comes to conversation
It's just the bees knees tops
Post office, groceries and butties to boot
With a good dollop of humour
You can have a right good hoot.

Christine Dickinson

MARTON MOSS IN WINTER

Frost crisp dawn,
Tree patterns embossed on sky,
Ground crackles, crunches, crumbles,
Stiff leaves remain, hedgerow hung,
Defiant of decay.

Branches ice-enamelled
Earth's slow breath distilled in cold crystal,
A myriad faceted reflections,
Ephemeral beauty, assimilating sun,
Dissolving in day.

Elva Knott

AN ODE TO PRESTON

Steeped in history is Priestown
Where priests went hiding underground
And Cromwell fought a battle or two
And the river Ribble runs right through
Once a busy working mill town
The chimneys and factories are all pulled down
No more green fields no cobbled streets
Just housing estates built big and neat
No corner shops or park with sand
The supermarkets have taken our land
It was nicer back then but now Preston's a City
Progress makes larger that's a real pity
Most things have changed even the name
But Lancashire dialect still says thi same
Thiv getten it reet about wat thi say
It was always much better back in my day.

Claire Cookson

ODE TO LANCASHIRE

I'm nowt burra Lancashire lass
I aint got very much brass
But Lancashire's the place tab be
I's wrote this ditty to make thee see
We has sky so blue and fields so green
A sea-side called Southport were thair is fresh and clean
Tis ere I love tab be
Gradely Lancashire folk means much to me
We have flers by roadside
Gerdens kept tidy and clean
If thi com from Souther England
Lancashire as to be seen
We have caws in field and orses too
When thi walks darn lane thi never feels blue
Ave ad mi ups and ave ad mi darns
Burra ave hallas farnd elp in Lancashire tarns
When chips are darn
And a'm flat on me ass
A'm so prade to be
A Lancashire Lass

Valerie Smith

MY HOSPICE

My home is in a dingy two bed tenement,
My life is down and out,
My wife is in in a hospice.
For those who have to live their life in a slum
In Deepdale, the Indian quarter
12 people to a 2 bed terrace.
My wife left for the bright lights in the city.
The council says things are improving
There are shops open and the jobs are near,
The ginnels are now cleaner, but
Is this the fate of all our homes?
Preston, my hospice, but
They say we are about to boom
The parks have won awards,
Christmas is drawing nearer.
Will we celebrate, or will we hate it
The weather is at least quite mild, not cold.
A solitary seagull flies over the docks, now derelict
Once busy now empty,
Is this the fate of Preston?

Stephen Alan Greasley

IN PASSING

Lancaster the tourists gem
As many ones have tried to pen
Lots for you to do and see
Most visitors they will agree
The castle and the priory church
With reputation you cannot besmirch
The museums from another time
Dolls general and maritime
Queen Victoria stands in Dalton Square
Stonewell changing place for a mare
Lord Ashton's memorial stands on a hill
With butterfly house to take your fill
Almshouses they are a pretty sight
And the Lune flowing on with all its might
Historical buildings all over the City
Some been demolished more is the pity
On outskirts it's country scenic and pretty
To one side its ocean the other the city
So visit and enjoy the delights to the full
You'll always have much information to mull.

Bob Harrison

HISTORIC LANCASTER

Salute the heroes of the past
That honed the mould from which we're cast.
As evolution wends its way,
From ancient times to present day,
Business has prospered and empires grow
And from their efforts riches flow.
But titans crumble and empires fall,
Like breaches to a city wall.
New enterprise to take their place
Are required at ever increasing pace.
Give praise to those with interests spread
Who provide the work to keep us fed.
In Lancaster the men abide
To take the future in its stride.
Salute the heroes from the past,
That honed the mould from which we're cast.

Donald Armitage

Born in Arthington near Leeds, **Donald Armitage** has interests including fell-walking and gardening. "I would describe my style as emotional and I would like to be remembered for my writing. My booklet of short poems *Furor Poeticus* is on sale at £5 from 4 Vicarage Close, Burton-in-Kendal, Carnforth, Lancashire, LA6 1NP, postage paid." Aged 78, Donald is retired and has ambitions to live happily with his wife Joyce and to remain healthy and active.

THE GARDEN PARTY

Saturday is the garden party
held at the URC manse,
no wooden flooring on the lawn
so afraid nowhere to dance.
We didn't seek an opener,
Lloyd Webber was discussed,
but he said "sorry, try Tim Rice
for he should be a must"
Alas poor Tim declined and said
that he was not available,
but if possible it would be nice
for a singer to go round each table
taking a turn to sing a few lines
from current shows in theatres.
and who better if she can be tempted
than Elaine Page synonymous with Evita.
Alas imagination of whom we might get
to do the introduction
has failed, but true to those on stage
for our folks the show must go on.

Joseph Alston

ORMSKIRK

Ormskirk, Ormskirk in its place, a nice little town
With its grace.
Every Saturday and Thursday too,
A market place for me and you, with bread and cheese
with fun galore, it remains so simple not much more.
Woolworths, Boots, Crazy Cards
All fun shops for kids at heart.
If a problem the bobby comes round,
He sorts it out with a tut and a frown.
We also have some famous treats,
Gingerbread men which are fun to eat.
Parish Church and New Church House,
Creating clubs for us kids to run about.
With services on a Sunday,
To end the week before next Monday.
And next about the tower and steeple,
And under them are the Ormskirk people.
So now to end this happy poem.
To go straight home
And snuggle up and think about the times I've had in town.

Holly White

ROSSENDALE VALLEY

A place not geographically refined
The elements can be so unkind
Living here without a brolly
To say the least is extreme folly.

Now its assets I will reveal
To most they are of some appeal
Strong boots, a haversack to go off hiking
Over tors, or gentler moors, as to your liking.

Skiing, swimming, football and cricket too
Many sports there are to do
For theatre goers we do provide
Local productions produced with pride.

Although not stamped with five star seals
Eating places abound with good food meals
People pause to pass the time of day
Manners not yet set in deep decay
We stick our chests out with some pride
In Rossendale, we've nowt to hide.

Allan Dixon

BLACKBURN SONG

Flocks of weavers came to stay,
spinning yarn in a special way
Breathing life into English soil,
working hard in the factory toil.

With the help of *Spinning Jenny*,
vast fortunes created by the many.
Terraced houses led to mills,
where workers sweat to pay their bills.

Families with children to the fore,
Amidst rattling sounds of each looms roar.
Friendships forged in yarn together,
spinning through a lifetime, lasting forever.

Our factory looms have all now gone.
But the smell of linseed will linger on.
New generations walk our mills,
shopping for bargains and other thrills.

Regeneration is now the rage as
Blackburn Town enters another age.

Isaac Livesey

THE MOSS EDGE ROAD

The low-slung coupé glides with easy grace
Along the narrow causeway.
Four cylinders in line three forty torque
Where once the patient horses slipped and strained,
Whilst carters cursed or murmured pious prayers.

This ancient road, as straight as mild steel bar,
I travel, west coast bound, as choice of route,
In soft green springs and winter's crisp white frosts,
The clouds a seagull grey towards the hills.
So year has followed year in feverish race,
To join the host of centuries gone before.

Sometimes, below the sound of singing tyres,
I seem to hear the growl of ancient ice,
The bellow of elk, the tread of hob-nailed soles,
The ring of burnished bronze of iron plate,
The crack of whips on countless market days,
The hiss of traction steam at harvest times.
And, clear above this hubbub from the past,
The laughter of lovers walking long ago
Under the high Fylde sky.

Albert Penty

LIVERPOOL, CITY OF LIGHT

At 7pm the journey ends
in harmony with light. - We exit -
from a glissando on the by-pass
forming miles of motorway. On dark tarmac
rear lamps glow, break, disintegrate
to red October dusk. In a steaming herd
one leading horn still moaning
disturbs the silence of an old eclipse. We listen
delayed by a traffic snarl
aware of a mirage rising
in the west.

No illusion but a northern town
lit up for the night. A tapering flare
of suburb
neon centre
outlying estuary.

Slowly we wind the windows down
hear only a largo on the wind.
Watch a brilliant city that stands for home
shed beauty and dignity.

Gina Riley

MEMORIES OF BURNLEY

Home from school
How I loved the dark dreary streets
The sooty smell
The tall chimneys
The cheery friendly voices
Back home love.

Our house was at the end of the street
Past the terraced houses
Fronted by stone steps and cobbles
Past the old ladies
Wrapped in black shawls
Feet in clogs
Back home love.

Oh the friendliness of those Burnley folk
Now time has travelled along
Gone are the tall chimneys, the noisy mills
Gone is our street, a car park now
But saddest of all
No longer a friendly call
Back home love.

Libby Grimes

Born in Burnley, **Libby Grimes** has interests including
collecting old books and antiques. "I would describe my
style as thoughtful and I would like to be remembered as
someone who cared," she pointed out. Aged 70, Libby is a
retired nurse. She is the widow of Geof and has three
children. "The person I would most like to meet is Tony
Benn. My biggest fantasy is world peace," added Libby.

FRAGILE FRIENDSHIP

We had a date,
But she was late.
I waited in the rain, in vain.
New Year's Eve two thousand and four;
She'd never been so late before.

I made my way towards her home;
Blinds drawn, she lived alone.
I was surprised, but surmised,
She'd just popped out,
To have her hair sorted out.

A neighbour noticed curtains closed.
I just supposed my friend had dozed.
She'd never been as late before.

Inside the house, upon the floor,
She clutched my hand, couldn't stand,
Murmured *Geoff.*
With barely breath.

Friendship: such a fragile flower;
All's well; at a stroke it's over.

Geoffrey W Lever

BARNOLDSWICK

Barnoldswick, for sixty years my home
From which I have no desire to roam
Surprising, really, from whence I came
An Eastern land! of sun, fun and game.

B'lick is gentle and kind, where else will I find
Friendly people on the town square
With whom to sit and pleasantries share.
Or enjoy a coffee in Victoria's caf!
And wave to my friends as they pass.

The shops close by are superb, indeed I do not jest
Believe me Chicken Harry's ham is the best
Home made cakes are always on request
Fish and chips, takeaways, a plenty
Pubs galore, posh restaurants, for higher gentry.

Don't cry for me Barnoldswick, the truth is
I'll never leave you, this town once of renown
For the rush, to live *o the brush,*
Strangers ask *where are we at?* Rolls Royce,
And Silentnight Industries are here
Need I say more than that.

Marie Keating

BURNLEY, MY HOME TOWN

Past pictures of Burnley to me
Full of smoke and not much to see
It's alright today
But back then it looked grey
I'm sure most folk would agree.

Dark looking shops
With small narrow streets
Burnley's now changed
And looks quite a treat
Coffee shops, walkways
And plenty of space
And still more development
About to take place.

So don't criticise all that you see
Things have to change so let it be
Please look at Burnley and judge on the whole
It's lost all the muck
But not lost it's soul.

Marie Smith

Dedicated to my sons - Julian, Philip and Kevin, with all my love.

SWEET LITTLE ANGEL

Our love for Megan was the strongest link,
As the whole church became a sea of pink -
Interspersed by greens, purples and blues,
In fact, lots of colours of varied hues.

She was a cheeky, cheerful little girl,
She changed our lives and put 'em in a whirl,
She enriched this world and made it better,
My only regret, I wish I'd met her.

But our memories of Megan will never die,
Fondly remembered with each tear in our eye,
As, alas the river of heartache will ne'er run dry,
As it constantly overflows with tears of, *why?*

Now there's a new star in the night sky,
That shines so brightly where the angels fly,
As we say in our hearts, with a heavy sigh,
Good night, God bless, Sweet Angel, goodbye.

Vincent McNicholas

*Dedicated to Megan Jayne Birchall - A sweet, little angel
taken too soon. She touched our hearts and souls forever.
God bless her.*

HOMELAND DESTROYED

This pain, this pain don't go away
It's with me always through each day
Relentless, searing, scorching me
It dims all joy that there could be.

My life goes on, my heart still beats
And every beat still beats for thee
The times we had, the love we shared
Now where are you, for no-one cares.

The life we had is gone for good
Torn apart by wanton thugs
Experts in the ethnic scene
Plucking seeds in case they breed.

My home is gone and so are they
Lost in hoards of souls displaced
Fleeing each and everyone
From death, destruction, rape and bomb.

What of the future, where to go?
No-one hears and no-one knows
How to find my children lost
Nothing is left, my hopes are dust.

Jean Emmett

RIVERSWAY DEVELOPMENT (PRESTON)

The Albert Edward Dock,
hewn from impervious bedrock,
opened for world-wide trade in 1892,
by Victorian forefathers, proud men and true.

Bustling and busy in its heyday,
wood pulp, grain, coals, oils and china clay,
from Windward Isles, Baltic and Scandinavian ports,
dock basin filled with calypso rhythms and banana boats.

Silting of channels, strikes and other reform,
led big ships sailing to other ports in the storm,
business dried-up, closure the last resort,
leading to dereliction and decline of this once proud port.

Out of industrial desolation,
the phoenix of regeneration,
from shattered warehouse debasement,
came the new Riversway Development.

Residential, retail and leisure,
Dockland's apartments of pleasure,
a lighthouse to lost shoppers' souls,
a marina to rival the Côte d' Azur's.

John B Townsley

MORNING MIST

The morning mist is all around
So crisp and fresh
Upon the ground
The autumn leaves drop from the trees
They look so bare
Just standing there.

But soon the buds
Once more appear
And then we know
That spring is here

Marjorie Riding

DARWEN MOORS

Alone on the top of Darwen Moors
Standing out like a beacon to all
It surveys it's town and everything around
Inviting everyone who makes the effort to call.

Many generations have climbed
Amazed by the view they behold
On a clear day young and old even find
Blackpool tower can be seen to unfold.

It's a venue for enjoyment for all,
On a warm day picnics abound and events
Take place all around
When cold it's encircled by mist
Giving it an eerie spiritual twist
What is the place surrounded by gorse?
Why Darwen Jubilee Tower of course.

Sheila Harper

MORECAMBE

Local poem, that's what the ad said,
As I talked to my best mate Fred.
What to say about my town.
A lot to think of, I'll be bound.

We could talk about the views
But usually it's the dog poos
The prom, the gardens, what a lark.
But on Sundays, it's a devil to park.

But on the whole, Morecambe's quite good.
And now of course, it doesn't flood.
It's on the way up, or so they say.
A bright light, shining across the bay.

I like living here, I hate to admit.
That's because I've been around a bit.
But each time that I come back.
I easily settle into my flat.

Now Fred doesn't say much,
He's a quiet sort of chap.
But so would you be.
If you were a cat.

Barbara Robinson

THE SYSTEM

Always under lock and key
In the systems no good for me
The only place that I can roam
Is in my mind but not my home

Blackburn born Burnley bred
My home is where I lay my head
From Eastern Clough to Flyde farm
My best friend now is self harm

Mary Burbury 5 years old
To the PICU unit feeling cold
Ward 11 Rossendale
Ward 18 my face is pale

I'm now on Bowland in Blackpool
Some may say a psychotic fool
With guild lodge they've threatened me
Another lock another key

Now back to Blackburn's where I'm going
I've got my paddle and yeah I'm rowing
So when you ask about my home
Don't be surprised if I just moan

Ben Lee Almond

THEATRE OPEN

Days fade into velvet nights
At the dimming of the lights,
Then the brilliance of a scene
Psychedelic blue and green.

Vital eyes express surprise
When the curtain starts to rise,
Noisy voices roistering
When the chorus starts to sing.

Fantasies will be fulfiled
Even when the music's stilled,
By the maestro's lowered hand
As he orchestrates the band.

Floating smoothly as a ship
Over waves will rise and dip,
Dancers catch a dream and then
Lightly toss it back again.

Stillness, then a mighty roar
As the audience shouts for more
Wondering if they have seen
Fantasies which might have been.

Nancy Reeves

LANCASHIRE LASS

I am a young Lancashire lass
From Preston - born and bred
Work nine till five to stay alive
But weekends are made for bed!

I am a young Lancashire lass
Who loves to watch her team
The lilywhites, come on the lads
To go up would be a dream

I am a young Lancashire lass
Who enjoys her pie and peas
But Friday night is *chippy* night
Lots of gravy please

I am a young Lancashire lass
Who lives her life to the full
I love old Lancashire sayings
My favourites *E by Gum*

I am a young Lancashire lass
And proud as you could be
Lancashire through and through
A Lancashire lass that's me!

Joanne Platt

LITTLE DONKEY

Little donkey, you're so sweet,
With your little donkey feet.
You follow your mama, whenever she moves,
Gingerly lifting your tiny hooves.

We love your coat; it feels like fluff;
It's softer than a powder puff.
We like to reach out to stroke your fur;
But when mamma is near, we need to mind her.

Because your mama's aware of all that's around;
Her ears are turned up to each and every sound.
If she thinks we're too close, when we're next to you,
We may get a warning, you know what she'll do.

She'll bunt her head at us, as if to say,
Leave my baby alone, you stay away!
So, we'll try to be careful, and we'll try to be slick;
We'll still give you a pat, even if it has to be quick.

Glenway

Glenway said: "I first developed a passion for writing in 2004. My first poem was written in appreciation of men and women who have served, or are currently serving in the military. Shortly after discovering a poetry workshop website, I found that reading and writing verse was a comfort during a difficult time in my life. I have had three short books of poems published. These are as follows: *Heart Strings and Butterfly Wings* available at www.amazon.com, www.barnesandnoble.com and www.publishamerica; and *Goodbye Snoopy* and *Letter To My Mentor* available at www.lulu.com."

PRESTON - MY TOWN

We've not much claim to fame or to fortune
For cotton and weft we're renowned.
For clogs and for shawls were the image
Of Prestonians and of their town.

Our charter it dates back to Henry
A guild we have each twenty years.
With egg rolling on Easter Monday
And I'm proud of the town I hold dear.

Our city boasts Finney and Flintoff
Two sportsmen that are of the best.
Yes, we can show them, in Preston
We sometimes outshine the rest.

Preston's flag's reached Australia
With the towns coat of arms, do you know?
With the lamb of St John the Baptist
With P P adorning below.

There's so much to tell about Preston
Come on down, just take a tour.
Find Arkwright, Robert Service, St Walburge's
Oh, and museums, stately buildings, much more.

Jean Turner

HERITAGE

Dirty old mill town,
where did you go?
Town of my birth,
How I miss you, so.

Gone are the chimnies,
Gone are the trams.
The once familiar,
Is now an alien land.

Gone are the flat caps,
Gone are the clogs.
Where is King Cotton?
He's gone to the dogs.

Gone are the cobbled streets,
Gone, the iron street lamps.
Replaced with ugly concrete,
Grey, lifeless and damp.

Bring back the heart,
Bring back the soul.
The town we remember,
A part of us all.

Kara Walmsley

NOSTALGIA

When I was a lad I didn't have a dad
He died sometime in the forties
There was me and my mum, we still carried on
While Bomber Command did their sorties

After the war we were still quite poor
But we lived not so bad on quite little
There's no use of moaning said my mum
We can't afford to be fickle

Around Gannow Top was my stamping ground
And Whittlefield Rec was my playground
We played football, cricket and went for walks
We didn't just hang around

I enjoyed my time in the early days
But things have changed a lot
With the Empress Ballroom, Vic and Arc's as well
These and lots more were quite hot

This is our borough our town of Burnley
With two rivers the Calder and Brun
They run through the town
Where once I had so much fun

Barrie Whittaker

TIME SHIFT

The village I live in was built on King Cotton
Though the era has gone it isn't forgotten,
Balmy summer mornings the visions appear
As if happening now and not yesteryear.
The knocker up raps on windowpane glass,
Clattering clogs on stone flags as they pass,
Fresh bread being baked at the top of our street
Wills me to get up for an oncoming treat.
Smells of mill smoke,the hiss of the steam
I awake, they've long gone, was it all but a dream?

Roy Hawkes

BONNIE COLNE

Bonnie Colne is known by name and really has its roll of
fame,
A modern street yet old it's sure the motto says we will
endure,
Yes enduring hills which way you go, Lenches, Knotts
Lane, and Valley Road,
But Colne has lots of fame Birtwhistle is one by name
A sinking ship, a bandsman plays as the ship goes down
In heavy sea he is playing, *Nearer My God To Thee*,
A massive flag that was laid by hand
And a church with stocks upon its land
To say a jam of good flavour by name in all the town
Does it seem the same even upside down
It also is a market town and history of mills and folk will
astound
This is the town of bonnie Colne my place of birth and
much renown.

Ena Barker

THE BANNISTER DOLL

A poem about Preston
Well I'll tell you one
I've lived her for yonks
Its history is second to none

The Banister doll's a good 'un
She's the ghost of Ladywell Street
The lass was tied to a lamppost and whipped
From her head to the soles of her feet

This rash decision by her daddy
Came about 'cause the girl was with child
Her kid's father of course was unknown
So John Bannister sort of went wild

Why did he kill his own daughter
Because the man could not live with the shame
Unknown to him the girl had been raped
But he just thought of his family's name

The suffering girl met her maker
She went like a lamb to the slaughter
Her father was told that after she died
He had murdered his innocent daughter

Jake Jackson

CLIMBING PENDLE

We are climbing up Pendle on a windy March day,
Her flanks white with snow up above,
The gale in our faces blows our troubles away,
As we walk on the hill that we love.

We are climbing up Pendle and gasping for breath,
Well, the one doing the gasping is me,
One minute elation the next, feels like death,
Wind blown tears mean I hardly can see.

We are standing on Pendle and gazing below
Over Clitheroe and Stonyhurst too,
Hearts beating like engines our faces aglow,
And spirits, that thrill to the view.

Now we are sliding down Pendle on stones covered with
snow,
Slipping and sliding our way,
I'm cursing my partner and he's laughing I know,
But oh! what a fantastic day.

We're sat in an alehouse, on Chatburn's main street
Each with a pint of Thwaites bitter,
My whole body is aching and I've got sore feet,
And I'm wishing that I were much fitter.

Kenneth Houghton

GARSTANG'S MILLENNIUM WINTER WALK

Now, on the Millennium walk, lone man and dog are to be
seen,
At one with nature, camouflaged, both in coats of waxy
green.

Cloaked in misty mournfulness the river Wyre trickles by,
The cold, grey of its icy depths, is mirrored in the frigid
sky.

All the trees are whipped and stripped by winter's hand
unkind,
Where all along the bridle path blows a biting easterly
wind.

And in the distance purple hills now topped with dust of
snow,
A beauty unseen by day trippers, all long gone by now.

A lone grey bush tailed squirrel scampers this and that
way,
Gathering nuts and berries red, to take back to his drey.

Despite these shortening half-light days of winter's bleak
necessity,
This place will always have and hold its own unique reality.

Dorothy Ellis

OLD LANCASHIRE LIFE

Lancashire looms went clickety clack,
The shuttles did fly, there was dust on their back.
The picking sticks picked, the weavers did weave.
There was dust in their lungs, they coughed and they
sneezed.

They worked for more pennies, from morning till night,
To put food on the table and a candle to light.
They lived in small houses, they were cold and were damp.
They tried to read books, by a small gas lamp.

The clothes that they had, were tattered and torn.
They worked at the mills, almost from the day they were born.
There was rickets, diptheria, their children were sick,
But still went to work, with a hoop and a stick.

The clogs on their feet, they were made out of wood.
As they walked to and from mill, it sounded so good.
But death came quite soon, in those Lancashire days.
But people were better, in all of their ways.

If I had to choose, between present and past.
With modern day cars, that travel so fast.
With drugs and with wars, and terrorists knife.
I know I would choose, old Lancashire life.

John Neil Ruffley

John Neil Ruffley said: "I am a retired plumber and I'm married to Margaret, with two sons and two grandchildren. I have been writing monologues and poems for many years on various subjects. Much of my work has a nostalgic theme whereas others are more humorous. In 1960 I began working as a plumber in Preston. At that time many of the cotton mills were operational and I was fortunate to work in them as a contract plumber. I have many memories of the mills and the characters who worked there. Consequently, these experiences have greatly influenced my writing."

THAT SHORT WORD - HOME

Home, a word to conjure up thoughts
So varied, more often so cruelly diverse
Where vile abuse lived, behind closed doors
Love never visited, family life just a curse

Physical, mental abuse, a common daily use
One movement, or one word sadly uttered
Thumps, kicks, threats of life quickly ending
Shouts for help - unheard, bloodily muttered

Babies, young children, undeservedly starved, alone
They know no different, truly think this is *home*
A life of squalor, human waste, dirt their friend
Never seeing daylight, thus here, their private zone

Believe me, this happens, maybe next door to you
Frightened to interfere, you don't need violent trouble
Your home perfectly pristine, severely well conducted
To *help* far too much, alas bursting your *bubble*

So many thousands of homes, where walls provide cover
Containing lives not worth living, evil reigns happily each
day
Naive souls reside here, their identities tragically unknown
Towns like this, like yours, harbour such places called
home

Maureen O'Hara

THE PLATTS LAKE DUCKS

I live in Burscough village
In a place called Thoroughgood Close
I've lived in many places
But I like this one the most.

My daughter baby Aimee
Likes to feed the Platts Lane ducks
And as we walk past Bargain Booze
She likes to count the trucks.

We sometimes take a picnic
And sit down by the lake
And say hello to passers by
Whilst munching on our cake.

I tell her every time we go
We're lucky to live near such a place
That can cheer you up when you're feeling down
And put the smile back on your face.

Of course she doesn't understand
Nor care - for her only worry
Is will we see the train go past?
"We might mummy if we hurry!"

Andrea Blease

Dedicated to my lovely daughter Aimee Lauren and my god-son, Cameron.

OUR TOWN

It took six days to make this world,
then he got to our town and took a day off
He also created our majestic Pennines
to remind us how tiny we compare
and girls that are bonny, as anywhere else.

Terrace houses survived industrial bondage
and those lads never returned from foreign fields.
Days of aroma of yeast from the brewery
the pong from the bone-yards, now gone the ways
of factory chimneys, defiling our skies.

Young 'uns don't know what hard times is
but our elders hardly had credit cards
tried driving through the town centre
parking longer than allowed, getting through lights
navigating mayhem, during school times.

Dregs of litter, *me first* attitudes
Because this is space age *dot com u c*
Telly-wellie, computers and kids that disobey
we now look forward with greater dreams
the future looks rosy but not for our team.

Keith Clegg

Born in Rawtenstall, **Keith Clegg** started writing poetry at school. "It has always been something I have enjoyed doing and my work is influenced by people. You can visit the four corners of the earth and you will never find two people exactly alike." he said. Aged 68, Keith is retired. He is married to Freda and they have one son, one daughter and three grandchildren. "I have written short stories and articles, and my biggest fantasy is to sing a duet with Katherine Jenkins. The person I'd most like to meet is David Beckham, providing he lends me his chequebook, if Victoria will let go of it!" added Keith.

BURNLEY NOW

There was a town of dark, satanic mills
Where the *knocker-up* wakened the people,
To tramp over the cobbles in their clogs
To run six looms and send cotton throughout the world.
Before lighting the fire and stoning the step.
That was long years ago when fish 'n chips
were a penny, if you had one.

What of Burnley now? A different town,
Visit a vibrant town centre
Sit out at a boulevard café drinking latté,
Or got to Burnley F C and celebrate with Bertie bee
And if you reach a certain age
After your swim, thanks to St Peter
Catch your free bus home from our new
purple palace bus station.
Or maybe visit Towneley Hall, our jewel in the crown
To remember how it was and to rejoice for today.

Eileen Naylor

LIVERPOOL

A place by a pool - that's called Liverpool,
With the liver-birds flying so high;
Where the Beatles grew up and all seemed so *cool*
To the sound of *Lucy in the Sky*.
A city that grew from Mersey trade,
A city of laughter and joy;
Where the ships sailed out and the people prayed
In churches both man and the boy.
Liverpool! It's a city for all,
A place full of life and romance;
Where the people walk tall and worship football,
While they laugh and they sing and they dance.
So for all who live here give a loud cheer,
A place that's been great from the start.
For a place we hold dear let's shed not a tear,
For a city that touches the heart.

Timothy Cunningham

CRASH AND BURN

As I left my home and walked to town
I walked the streets and gave a frown
For once again the scals had smashed the bus station
Why is this nation
So destructive and full of alienation?

When I got to town I saw the litter cluttering up the street
But I felt slightly happier for I saw
One of the few respectful citizens put his tin
In the almost empty bin
However my smile soon left
When I saw the charity shop empty due to theft
How could someone steal from charity?

Liverpool will crash and burn
If this does not take a turn
Forget the myth of the Liverbirds flying away
Liverpool will destroy itself to my dismay.

                                          Jack Lindon

LIVERPOOL

Different cultures, many races and all one society,
Bringing us together, black or white, big or small,
Liverpool is for one and all.

Welcoming weary sailors to our shores,
Enjoying the city of culture and the people.

The football fanatics, jolly jokers, merry men and women,
Many folks pass and gaze at our city's sheer excellence,
It is an oasis in a desert.

A peaceful, tranquil area when the world is in war.
When people are attacked and killed for narrow
Mindedness,
Remember you will never walk alone in Liverpool.

Out of all these good things there is one bad,
The day Liverbird falls Liverpool will cease to exist.

Ron Sen

THE ROAD FROM AINSDALE TO HALSALL

I love the narrow road across the moss.
Black above the flat green stretch of fields,
Above the deep, uneasy darkness of the ditches.

I love the summer sunburst of the rape seed yellow,
The white spring froth of cow parsley,
The sharp green stalks of winter wheat
And paler spikes of onion rows.

I love the straightness of the road through fields,
And yet the way it bends round house and farmyard
Above the waves of ordered green,
That wash around the island coverts
Where pheasants cower from glorious August guns.

When sunlight slants with evening gentleness
Or rain lies puddled in the grass,
Shades of green beside the tarmac's shiny black,
I love the road across the moss.

Joan Pyrke

SOUTHPORT FLOWER SHOW

Foundations are laid and holes are dug,
A quick drink of tea, from an enamel mug.
Tents are erected, to display cut flowers,
Digging the ground for hours and hours.

Putting in rocks, gravel and stone,
Each of the gardens are on the guide shown.
Signs are put up to show people the way,
Organisers, participants, for good weather will pray.

Southport flower show, a magnificent event,
With freshly made gardens and cut flowers in a tent.
Thousands of people, expected each day,
Hoping it's sunny and the rain stays away.

Brian Williams

LIVERPOOL

Oh Liverpool Liverpool
They name it twice
Oh beautiful city that
Lights in the night

We're so proud of three
Graces that stand so fine
And white
They even made it a
Heritage site

Being a scouser I am
So proud
This city of culture
Is coming around

Trevor Jones

FORMBY

Formby, home of nature,
Formby, home of war,
Formby holds two armies,
The small falls to the floor.

David versus Goliath,
Big versus small,
The outcome's always the same,
Large wins them all.

One side is dying,
Quite literally I say,
If it is not stopped,
They'll be extinct one day.

Formby home of nature,
Formby home of war,
Formby holds the red squirrel,
Who need to be saved I'm sure

Andrew Smith

SOUTHPORT

I always enjoy Southport
And loved it as a child
Its shops, marine lake and candy floss
Great funfair with its rides

Lord Street with its flowers and cafés
A boulevard with style
Victorian architecture everywhere
Makes a visit so worthwhile

The pier goes on forever
Its seafront draws the crowds
A super flower show in August
Red arrows touch the clouds

So when you visit the Northwest
Make Southport a place to see
You will love the air and the people
It's never never disappointed me

Brian Lally

WHY ROAM, STAY HOME

Let's relax and have a stroll
Along the Albert Dock.
Forget all woes and worries!
Look at that splendid clock.
Let's stay at home in Liverpool,
We never do feel bored:
As capital of culture
No need to go abroad.
By ship across the Mersey
We breathe the fresh sea-air.
Liverpudlians love to tan
And some like stripping bare.
Now let's have a shopping spree
As we go into town,
We'll visit our cathedrals -
They both deserve a crown!
Scousers are so football mad
They'll go to lots of trouble.
Relax, enjoy yourself and soon
They'll give a friendly cuddle.

Jean Jones

VISION

To see is the need for far and away
The feel of the ocean the more is to pray
Sight, sound all the more great
But the feeling of touch, a sinner so late
Movement and power to relish the thought
But a steady hand is upon that blossom court
Purity and fire alive with hope
Death and destruction can only elope
Heaven again the gates of passion
Let them seek all that has happened
To take thee so neutral and cold
They want not only
Must be, to hold

Graham Collum

CITY SONNET

The early morning city wakes again
As cleaners sweep the still-deserted streets;
A watery moon the cold, pale daylight meets
On pavements washed by a night of heavy rain.
Pigeons and gulls strut on the silent roads;
Tidal water slaps round sleeping boats
And an early ferry across the river floats,
While inland, trucks discharge their daily loads.
Then screeching buses and hooting taxis drive
Into the bustling city, now alive -
Sleepers from doorway beds have been awoken -
And, heads down to the wind, commuters walk
The weary route to office, bank and chalk,
For the deep voice of the town's giant clock has spoken.

Judith Hinds

LIVERPOOL

Liverpool is the place to be,
We've friendly people and much to see.
The giant buildings, the modern art,
The Merseyside River, where do I start?
The lambanana, the Albert Dock,
The radio city tower, we have a lot.

Liverpool, Everton, The Beatles, all stars,
Smashing football and smashing guitars.
Anfield Stadium, The Cavern Club,
The fans, the noise that we all love.
Slide tackles, complicated notes,
Liverpool get my vote.

University of Liverpool, Hope, John Moores,
Come as a tourist, sight-see and take tours.
Liverpool College, Blue Coat and Belvedere,
Actually come and stay here.
Capital of culture, isn't it great,
It's all kicking off in 2008!

Matthew Jung

LIVERPOOL

At school a reluctant poet, it was not my art
But when it comes to my hometown,
This comes right from my heart
We got the capital of culture 2008
With visitors from all over the world
Won't it be great?
We are the home of The Beatles
Get yourself to Matthew Street
With sounds of the 60's,
Everyone loves to dance to that beat
All over the world, we are known for both football teams
And down the years both our players
And the Fab Four have brought on many screams
There's so much to see and loads to do
If you're into cathedrals?
Hey, we've got two
The scousers will make you welcome
With never so much as a frown
And the *last* thing you will hear
Is *Calm down, lah, calm down!*

Carol Houghton

MY FAVOURITE PLACE

Southport is home to me
Favourite places here to see.
Grey stone fountains look continental
Cascading water is ornamental.
Many shops are in our town
Busy traffic up and down.
Taxi cabs and buses stop
Bringing people in to shop.
Lots of pubs in which to eat
Restaurants also for a treat.
Choice of food, exotic or plain
Television has brought some fame.
The Marine Lake is a peaceful place
Setting a different quiet pace.
Putting, golf, train and boat
Steamer and row boats all afloat.
Tides around do ebb and flow
As the seasons come and go.
The new pier takes you to the sea
Making Southport the place to be.

Diane Horscroft

OFF SEASON IN ST IVES

The doors are closed the blinds are down
Streets are empty. Everyone has left the town
An eerie chill wind takes away my breath
It's off season and it seems like death

Walking along a rainy beach the beauty has all gone
I sit on a patch of sand come summer all will be on
But now nobody wants this place and so it is mine
But I'll be gone when everybody else has their time

Lunch in a diner the owner comes up to me
He says *It's off season everything's shut can't you see*
In summer you won't be able to hear yourself think for the
sound of tills
Taking money to pay outstanding *off season* bills

So roll on summer and quickly end your long days
And return next year in your inevitable way
I'll welcome back those dark gloomy nights
And will be free of the brash touristic sights

Peter Jones

LIVERPOOL - THE WORLD IN ONE CITY

A little bit of everything,
Some might say,
The world in one city,
A new adventure everyday.

Walking along the river front,
Or clubbing all night long,
In this heaven on earth,
Nothing can go wrong.

The city never sleeps,
Even when the sun goes down,
It's always buzzing,
In the centre of town.

The passion in the crowds at the footy games,
Always makes me smile,
And when you pour out of the Anfield gates,
Red and white is the style.

City life will take over you,
It will leave you wanting more,
Make sure you keep it close to your heart,
Because Liverpool is a place worth fighting for!

Leila Rooney

Born in Liverpool, **Leila Rooney** has interests including rock
and metal music, concerts and travelling. "I started writing
poetry at a very early age, encouraged by my teachers and my
father," she explained. "My work is influenced by my environ-
ment and my experiences, and I would like to be remembered
as
someone who thought that writing should be interesting and
fun for the reader, as well as a pleasure for the author." Leila
has an ambition to be a psychologist. She has written song
lyrics, many poems and some stories.

NEIGHBOURHOOD

I visited my old neighbourhood
I found it to be quite sad
Gone are the streets and houses
In Bootle where I grew up as a lad
The community had been torn apart
Friends and neighbours alike
Bootle isn't the same anymore
Where I played and rode on my bike
I remember back then
The way things used to be
None of us ever had very much
But there was a great camaraderie
Games were played in the street
Without fear of being chased away
Sometimes the parents joined in too
It was like that in my young day
But times have changed
And with it has gone
All the games that we played
That gave us children fun

Thomas Minshull

OUR PIT

They shut down our pit like it never mattered,
Not caring about lives that they ruined and shattered,
Thousands of jobs that just came and went,
Politicians not bothering at the living just spent,
We were working relentless as we toiled for our bosses,
Who had no regard as we counted our losses.

They took away work that was economically sound,
And left years of work that was still underground,
Getting people off the dole is their loudest shout,
After shutting our pit and keeping good workmen out,
Look back at the pits and see what went on,
As politics took over and common sense was gone.

The people who did it must now look back,
Realising the wrong when they gave us the sack,
They'll not admit it, they don't make mistakes,
Buying coal from abroad is all that it takes
We lost the fight but we never gave in,
They can only hope now, that God will forgive them their
sin.

Les Woods

SOUTHPORT SUNSET

Angry indigo clouds loom low in a bloody sky,
While across the sinking sun the screaming seagulls fly,
Silhouetted against the garish scene.
The struts of the marine bridge reach into the twilight,
Close by, the wooden pier accompanies it to the sea,
Dotted with twinkling light
And couples stroll like shadows down its planks
As the seagulls dip from the burning sky
Landing at the farthest point in ranks
And I love this place, it is my town and home to me.
Racing the sinking sun to the beach
I stand and watch the disappearing sea
Leaving the sands behind and whispering softly to me.

Frankie Shepherd

BEAUTIFUL BIRD

A beautiful bird looks over my city,
People say it looks bold, but some say it's pretty.
It looks over the Mersey and out to the town,
Folk say if you look closely it wears a frown.
Now that I'm not sure about, as this place is the best,
For all its singing and dancing,
And the world knows us for the rest!
Our sense of humour is second to none
And ask us a favour and it's already done.
We've a sense of good fortune,
Although some have nought,
But we share with our neighbours when there is a drought.
We're a pool of optimists,
A great big family affair,
So don't skit our accent,
Just don't you dare!

Sally-Ann Davies

SOUTHPORT - WITH LOVE

Remember those bikes the whole family could ride
And the hovercraft trips to Blackpool we'd glide
Striped orange blankets on the back of Red Rum
Cockles and shrimps to our shores they'd come

Ice cream, hot Vimto we'd have down at Rossi's
Amusement arcades, counting winnings or losses!
The land of little people, The Victoria Baths,
The Outdoor pool, we had so many laughs!

Old family firms such as Huytons' and Hewitts'
The factory made sweets but were famous for Chewitts
Saturday morning cinema, at the old ABC
Pie, chips and gravy from The Swan for my tea!

We all went to see them, and no family could deny
Showaddywaddy the rock band! Oh my, oh my, oh why!
The Big Dipper and Speedway, the rides at the fair
Are sadly no more and they're no longer there

Some childhood memories I've enjoyed these above
And I smile and I'm thankful, from - *Southport with love*

Jackie Marsh

LIVERPOOL

Liverpool city, my home town,
With people so caring they won't let you down.
The buildings and architecture are a sight to behold,
Where behind closed doors their treasures unfold.
Majestic cathedrals we have two,
Where all are welcome to wander through.
Cafes and pubs where people can meet,
Tucked around corners on every street.
Theatres present us with wonderful nights,
From ballet to Shakespeare and musical delights.
Down at the dockside history abounds,
The quayside is vibrant with colours and sounds.
Museums and galleries some old and some new,
Are a window to past life for me and for you.
Liverpool city a town with two teams,
The blues and the reds in the theatre of dreams.
Liverpool city what more can I say,
It's a city who's heart beats by night and by day.
When you're in Liverpool you're never alone,
It's the city, my city I'm proud to call home.

Joan Rawcliffe

Dedicated to my sister Josie, always remembered with love.

THE PALACE ICE RINK

The *Palace Ice Rink* was a famous landmark, and almost as popular as old *Princes Park*.
Skaters came from near and far, to visit the Palace, which was Fairfield's star.
Rich and poor, and the famous too, they would skate the evening through.
This was in the days when Liverpool was at its peak, and the standard of entertainment
was really quite unique, but since the city has declined, so the outlook is less refined.
Sadly the *Palace* has joined the list, of other joys that are missed.

Thomas McCabe

LIVERPOOL

Inside the Anglican, total silence apart from the wind
Blowing harshly into the cathedral
The sun shines brightly up the pew,
The Mersey reeking like last week's stew.

The shops are busy with people frantically rushing about
Yet there are some people who will stay at home and pout
For today Liverpool did not win so they'll create an awful din
Oh! What a sin! To deny Liverpool a win.

The Superlambanana stands still like a beacon of fire
Inspiring Liverpudlians passing by.
The pigeons covered in grey feathers like minute rocks
Floating in the sky.
Oh hooray! I'm in Liverpool today. I really hope you can stay.

Gabriel McNeilly

A TOUR OF LIVERPOOL

In town where Liverpool is love,
Full of friendly folk,
Who like having a good joke!
The art is the greatest,
Culture is the capital here in 08
With the Lamb banana and all.
The shopping is hot,
But the museums are not.
The cafes are fantastic,
The toys from John Lewis are plastic.

Now into the suburbs,
To Allerton supporting our local shops,
Going down Penny Lane, to see the magical Mystery Tour,
Cameras at the ready, then to the wigs in the Wiggins
shop,
Then last place of all down to Mather Avenue to the
monstrous Tesco, need to buy some pesto,
I hear a bang! The astro is ruined
The Tesco is getting bigger. Help! The monster is out.
Now we have come to the end of our swift tour,
Thank you and goodnight.

Lucy Sellars

LIVERPOOL: A TIME AND PLACE

From Jericho Farm to the Cast Iron Shore
The oil pipes and golf links are now no more
The overhead railway running from Dingle Mount Station
Viewed docklands that were once the pride of a nation.

This city that had seen continued decline
Has never been beaten and is now back on line.
We have monuments of architecture not found elsewhere
That are only surpassed by the peoples' great care.

The revival of Liverpool is beyond any doubt
Enterprise is as alive as within as without
Ghetto's a word that doesn't apply
The rehousing programmes can be seen by the eye.

Those great merchant houses abandoned in the past
Now form homes designed to last.

We have two football teams of world renown
As are the Beatles and the Cavern in town.
The hospitality and kindness of scousers abound
While the great sense of humour makes laughter resound.

Ronald A Crabtree

MY EVERTON STREET

There at the end of our cobbled street
there's an old funny bollard we used as a seat
We'd play two balls on the old brick wall
We'd run, chase, trip and fall
We'd play hide and seek and *off ground tick*
We'd sometimes squabble, fight and kick
We'd go on bikes to the Ten o'Clock store
spending pocket money on sweets galore
Sherbet, lollies, colas that crunch
Quavers, Fries, Monster Munch
There we'd be at the end of our street
on the old funny bollard we used as a seat
We'd play with our dog who would bark and scratch
We'd throw our ball, he'd jump and catch
We'd skip together on one long rope
singing rhymes full of hope
We'd play with dolls playing *Mum* and *House*
and wait for the call for our warm pan of scouse
There we'd be at the end of our street
on the funny old bollard that we used as a seat.

Wendy Black

*Dedicated to Eileen Miller for her friendship, encouragement
and support through the years.*

LIVERPOOL

Liverpool oh Liverpool,
It is the place to be, especially within the city.
When 2008 comes we will be the capital of culture.
And the best we will be!
Up in Liverpool, in the north west,
We have a good view over the rest.
Next to the Mersey we can see all the boat races,
A good place to be.
The winners and losers for what we see
Like to party on the quay.

Julien Toh

LIVERPOOL

As I walk down Liverpool Street,
The place I call my home,
Where all The Beatles lived before,
But now most unknown,
With yellow sheep roaming streets,
And green birds up high,
We hope that they don't leave us,
As Liverpool will sink and die,
I still love my Liverpool home
And how the city glows,
Liverpool is a special place
As every scouser knows.

Rose Maher

MY TOWN

In my part of Liverpool town
There's no wavin' trees, a curious scented breeze
Housin' estate waitin' to be pulled down
In my part of Liverpool town

In my part of Liverpool town
Graffiti walls broadcastin' a threat
To someone they'll meet but not yet
In my part of Liverpool town

In my part of Liverpool town
Birds chattle, stray dogs battle
A lawnmower drone of a chore
Distant screams, choice words
You don't live 'ere anymore

In my part of Liverpool town
It's where I was born and bred
It's where my children play, it's where I was wed
Here is no garden of Eden
It is my paradise
Couldn't leave for any price
From my part of Liverpool town

Paddy McCarty

LEASOWE

There is a place called Leasowe
Where I have my home
An estate run by the council
As you might have known

Most places have front gardens
And also out back too
There are some exceptions
But they are very few

We are quite near the ocean
To be true, the Irish sea
The hills of sand and sea grass
Will fill your heart with glee

It is a great peninsula
With water all around
You leave this place to wander
But soon you're homeward bound

We have beaches, shops and woodland
And a motorway straight through
There are other pretty places
But no other place for me will do

Andrew C Chapman

SOUTHPORT - 1960's

Bedrooms - eleven - and all of them full
Cooking for forty, with never a lull
Moments of madness, but none of them dull
Pray that the days will be sunny.

Hundreds of cases to haul up the stairs
Doubles and singles and ladies in pairs
Kids making sand-pies on sofas, who cares?
Laugh and pretend that it's funny.

Bolton week, Bury week, Nelson and Colne
Some with their children and some on their own
All of them hoping to gain half a stone
Getting good value for money.

Flower show week - they admire every stand
Sitting in deckchairs enjoying the band
English Rose finalists - all picked by hand
Each of them cute as a bunny.

Holiday finished, they brushed off a tear
Ending the week with a walk on the pier
Dreaming already of coming next year
In Southport, it's all milk and honey!

Dorothy Crossley

LIVERPOOL

My home town Liverpool
Is totally fabulously cool
It has lots of sights to see
Which really entertain me
In town and Albert Docks
There are some very nice shops
The Anglican Cathedral standing there
Proudly with its head in the air
People watch their football teams
And oh, how mad they seem
Then there's the Liver Bird
Which is very well known and heard
A group called The Beatles who were great
Everyone went to see them with a mate
Liverpool is a great city alone
It's my life and my home

Emma Richardson

Emma Richardson said: "I wrote this poem during an
English lesson at school. I love to write stories and poems
and my inspiration for this poem was my home city, of
which I am very proud. This is the second piece of my work
which has been published in the past two years. I live at
home with my mum, dad and elder brother, and my
hobbies include swimming, reading, socialising with friends
and listening to my favourite music."

THE SANDS OF TIME

When I think of Formby and dream of home,
I think of the sea and shimmering foam,
Wildfowl, rabbits and the natterjack toad,
Who ventures out at night, wily and bold.

Take time to visit Freshfield and the nature reserve,
A natural habitat the squirrels deserve.
The vibrant butterflies flutter past
And settle gently in the marram grass.

'Tis a Viking coast set in time,
With beautiful sand dunes line after line
An abundance of footprints lead down to the sea.
A wonderful haven; *The Land of Fornebi.*

Many visit just for the day,
Some to paddle and some to play,
All sorts of people shape our town,
Ordinary folk and some of renown.

If you fancy, take a sail on Liverpool Bay,
A place of culture or so they say!
So when you espy a forest of pine.
Remember with fondness *The Sands of Time.*

Janet Ashton

A PAINTING OF LIVERPOOL

If I could paint a picture
I'd do it now for you,
We'll walk the streets of Liverpool
And meet the people too

The Beatles at the Cavern Club
Create the famous Mersey Beat
And see Eleanor Rigby
Outside, she has her own seat

Ken Dodd, he lives in Knotty Ash
Not very far from me
The Butty Mines are here as well
With Diddy Men to see

The Albert Dock is not that far
See it all, for free
The waterfront and shops around
Pop inside the Tate Gallery?

I hope I have portrayed for you
The Liverpool I know best
Please feel free to call again
This place - far better than the rest.

Joan Jackson

FISHING

And now the time has come for me
To cast my nets, and fish the sea
They come aboard all flap and flip
Some can sting, and others give a nip
All aboard we give them room
Upon my ships in barrels soon
Then time and tide will take us back ag'en
To shores and beaches dale and fen
Where silver and gold are waiting there
For the selling and eating of our ware

Albert Carpenter

LIVERPOOL

Liverpool is the best city and has all the power
The cathedral, the shops and the radio city tower
The tourism is also great
Go and have a cup of coffee in the wonderful Tate
Go and listen to The Beatles in all of the bars
There are also lots of feminine spas
A big range of music something for all
Rock, R'n'B they're all on the wall
The fashion's outrageous so much to see
Goths, Emos and even me
Liverpool, Everton, we've got the best
Juniors, seniors we've also got the rest
There's a big yellow thing called The Lamb Banana
Thank God it wasn't made as a piranha
And as for the Mersey well that's just brown
No wonder when people look they just frown
Well that's my city, good old Liverpool
I think it's boss I think it's cool

Jane Bazley-Harrison

DOWN SOUTHPORT PIER

Beneath its tent the carousel begins
It's a wild kaleidoscope of gold and cream:
Leaping horses and white knuckle riders
Whirling ever faster as the music swells.
To the north the new bridge towers,
A massive lyre that waits the touch of a gigantic hand.
I wander under arching lamps and almost feel
The long pier, striding the bright sands
Into the ebbing tide.
Gulls hang motionless beside my elbow
Grey-white ghosts whose eerie crying haunts the breeze.
On rusting rails the bulging pier train crawls,
Its bleeper elbowing aside the crowd
That paces, ambles, loiters over brass plaque boards.
Ahead, the angular pavilion,
Green glass leaning hard into the wind,
There, Southport's past and future meet, as children
Clutching antique pennies in excited hands
Crowd the ancient slot machines.
Returning anglers trudge the weary timbers,
Faces downcast by the fishless day.
Looking back I see
A row of pearly buildings grinning white
And Southport smiles at me.

Philip Rowe

HOMEWARD BOUND

I have travelled far and wide
Took all the sites in my stride
It started with camp USA
I set off travelling on a sunny day

Back home I had itchy feet
So moved to Canada in one sweep
I did think about life back home
But didn't miss it or feel alone

When my time was up I travelled back
I was happy and that was that
Rainford Village not changed one bit
Local shops, small streets dimly lit

Next Liverpool like when I did my degree
The shops and the nightlife were just for me
A stroll around the Albert Dock is extremely pretty
There was always a glow and buzz in the City

But life is too short to sit in one place
A trip round the world stared me in the face
The best year of my life, achieving dreams
Now I am home for good or so it seems

Melanie Robinson

POEM

The football in Liverpool is so great.
City of culture in 2008.
In the city centre is the Liverpool eye.
Look at the Liverbirds up in the sky.
The boats come in at the Albert Dock.
In the Cavern Club the Beatles rock.
Liverpool is the greatest city in history.
I live in Liverpool.
The best place to be.

Ross Bagnall

SEASIDE TOWN

Southport is a seaside town,
Beaches, boats, trams, fairs, music, laughter, come on down.
Southport is packed with history,
Southport is covered in hidden mystery.
Plant life, wildlife and human life,
Like the weather it's running rife.
On the Marine Lake the swans have an air of great serenity
Like us they are ready to defend their territory,
Day to day life is a continual struggle for all,
We have to find food, shelter and stay out of danger's call
But there are moments of peace when sat upon the pier,
Remembering the good old days, love, warmth, thrills and spills that brought many a tear,
Flower shows, pantomimes, motor rallys, concerts to name but a few.
We are lucky to witness and proud through and through
Remember *old* Southport.
We are the best in Southport.

Brenda Marshman

BIRKENHEAD: THE SEA, THE WAR

Birkenhead was a busy port
When shipbuilding was at the fore.

Ships built by the dozen, men watched with pride
As those ships were launched, *hurrah*, they cried.

The story of those merchant sailors are those of courage
and pride,
Of the flag they sailed under, companions side by side.

Large ships taking passengers to exotic shores
Then it all changed, those ships went to a terrible war.

My uncle was on a merchant ship working down below,
He didn't stand a chance when the torpedoes blew.

The North Atlantic was where he died,
Not many on his ship survived.

Three merchant ships sank that awful grim night,
When memories still make father's tears flow.

Families waited by the dockside for the survivors to come
home
But for my family, they went home alone.

Susan Mansell

VORTEX

Park observatory on small hill
Black bin bags, icy cold wind.
Despite brilliant sun, gathering speed,
Magnificent!
Four kids, one daft mum.

Sparkling droplets of gold and silver
Cascade from weeping willow fountains
Onto the irregular shaped lake.

Southport has many beautiful places
Of that I must confess,
Yet, Hesketh Park is the best.
Trees abundant, nature trimmed
But not contained.
Lots of nooks and crannies to explore.

Round and round the oval perimeter
We all go.
Faces changing like the seasons
With the passing of the years.
Swirling images of the past
All caught in a vortex of time.

Marie Black

*Dedicated to my eldest son Steven for all the happy times,
both past and present. Love always, Mum.*

LIVERPOOL POEM

Liverpool has the Liverbirds,
Looking over us like a vulture,
One to the Mersey, one to the land,
And we'll soon be the Capital of Culture,
We also have the Cathedral
Been around for a long time,
It's part of our rich history,
Like Christmas with mistletoe and wine.

Adam Scanlon

SOUTHPORT

I like it when, on dark blue winter nights,
Christmas shoppers throng Lord Street and the lights
Are twinkling in the trees.

I love to see the first sail boats of spring
On the Marine Lake, like birds on the wing
They swoop and dip and fly.

Summer's the drama of the Flower Show,
The herbaceous pageant of Rotten Row,
New mown grass on the breeze.

But it is the autumn I like the best
When the salty winds blow in from the west
And wild geese fill the sky.

A town for all seasons?
Yes. Here are my reasons
Why Southport is special.

Andrea Rollins

THE RAINHILL TRIALS

It happened on a stretch of track
Where I now journey daily to Liverpool and back,

Novelty, Rocket and Sans Pareil, Perseverence, and
Cycloped
Powered by a horse that fell, a strange contraption it
should be said!
Shaking and rattling, billowing steam
Twenty journeys the ultimate dream

Sans Pareil made a promising start, ironic his chance of
survival
Depended on a boiler part provided by a rival
Novelty was small and light but slowly overheated
Started off like dynamite then suddenly hissed to a halt,
defeated!
Perseverance made his debut late for a mishap on the way
Was soon to seal this engine's fate as he missed the
starting day

The triumphant one was quite a toiler, spectacular, unique
With his multi-tubular boiler he became a star that week
To deafening cheers as he steamed out of sight the
winnings went in the pocket
Of a man who looked on with pride and delight,
Stephenson for his *Rocket*

Pauline Williams

MEMORIES OF AN ADOPTED TOWN

I lived up north where the wind blew cold,
With my family and friends and peoples of old.

Then one day I heard, right out of the blue,
I was going to Wales and pastures new!

When I moved my eyes beamed delight,
The town was called Neath, a welcoming sight!

I made many friends in that little old town.
The Welsh lady in costume, so gracious her gown!

Bora Da my lovely girl she would announce with a smile
Which I returned with a *Good morning*,
But, oh, I did like her style.

Folk sang in their choirs, so rich was their song,
I felt the mountains behind me rise to the throng.

Calon Lan was my favourite, I would practice so hard,
But my northern roots forbade me
From conquering their art.

Memories of home are now of my Neath,
A place of beauty, tranquillity and the
Call of the Heath.

Carole Ginty

HOMESTEAD

No slowly dying seaside town is this my birthplace home,
Chameleon town of many faces,
Some harking back to days long gone, yet others brave and
bold,
Reaching out fresh tendrils into modernity.

Townsfolk and tourists, made idle by the Indian summer
Perambulate the Victoria parade,
Stroll the pier and gather in clusters of white-shorted
languor
On the velvet parkland.

Children gallop their steeds on the carousel,
Bright eyes shining and their hair streaming out.
Those too young to ride, watch on,
Small tongues licking pink and white ices, and sticky pink
clouds on sticks.

Fraternities of ducks navigate the swan clogged lake,
Trying to gain the glassy calm beyond the throng.
A phalanx of geese fly high,
Their haunting autumn call echoing on the wind.

Whilst I sit tranquil, the whole beach prostrate before me,
Distant ocean sliver glinting through the haze.
The cacophony of gulls rips the silence
As the molten red sun slinks into the shimmer.

Anna Hindmarch

AULD BASS ROCK

The sun shines on auld Bass Rock.
Majestic, invincible fortress
A kingdom for many thousands
Of clackering, chattering, greedy gannets,
Who cause this ancient giant's hair
To become as white as snow
Until they go
Those greedy gannets, clackering and chattering
To warmer clime.
Leaving auld Bass Rock
To a quieter time.
A slumbering lion
Sinking and sighing into winter sojourn
Left to brood alone
Until the gannets return
To breed and groan
And race for space,
Which auld Bass Rock shares,
A smile on his face.

Ann Tregenza

WELCOME

Sunny Southport, sand and sea, all waiting here for you.
The boulevards so beautiful, the buildings old and new.
Join with the past, to delight your eye, a magnificent bridge and pier.
A delightful town, refreshing air, you'll enjoy every moment here.

Fine dining, shopping, theatre, shows, top billing of stars you know.
Flower show, air-show, yachts and cars, great parks and gardens on show.
A holiday here will fill the bill, it needn't cost the earth.
Sailing, swimming, walking, dancing, all have tremendous worth.

Golfing, fishing, all kinds of deals will delight professional folks.
There isn't anything you can't find here. Even street shows, and jokes
Like the sea being gone, not strictly true. Tides come and go every day.
Relax, have fun with never a care. Golden sands, where kids safely play.

Every kind of venue to suit yourself; village pubs, great food, great fun.
Come to Southport, have a drink on us,
For a warm welcome.

Dorothy Gerrard

LIVERPOOL

Liverpool, a cultured city,
Capital of culture 2008,
With magnificent architecture
And brilliant musicians.

Two huge cathedrals, towering over us all,
The Anglican, as tall as a mountain,
The Roman Catholic, dwarfing us all.
Two monolithic wonders.

The Beatles, worldwide legends,
Heard all over the world
Playing in the Cavern.
True heroes of Liverpool.

Ian Dorrington

SOUTHPORT

Why not come to Southport and have some family fun,
Where you could meet the old and the young without
having a pun.
The elderly are not just like gnomes,
As they don't just sit in their retirement homes.
I wonder why Southport makes them so frisk,
Is it the clean air or the fun they have missed?
This is the town that should be renowned for the fun of the
fair,
And not just an armchair.
The food connoisseur is second to none,
Even the fish and chips have beaten rivals from everyone.
Southport is getting stronger and stronger,
With whole family events makes a remembrance last a lot
longer.
I know I will never forget,
Every time I visited the town a celebrity I have met.

Kenneth Thompson

A SANDGROUNDER

The sandgrounder on the photograph
Was called Joe Rimmer -
He was sitting on a shrimper's cart
Staring at me from a postcard -
That was when life was hard
In days gone by in Southport.
Now this town is buzzing with bistros
And wonderful shops -
Bright lights twinkle in tree lined Lord Street
And in the distance seagulls cry -
Searching for shrimps that lie
Across the sand in shallow waters.
I once saw horseshoe prints in the sand
And ridges made from cartwheels
Did I see the ghost of Joe Rimmer I wondered?
As I walked barefoot along the edge of the sea -
Deserted sands and only me -
A sandgrounder in Southport.

Gillie Bishop

ANOTHER PLACE

One hundred iron men stand on the sand of Crosby shore,
I've never seen such a sight before.
But the burning question of the day is
Will they be allowed to stay?
Some locals are saying send them away!
But I should like to have a say.
When Pharaoh Khafre put the Sphinx
Upon the sand in Egypt long ago, no one there
Said it had to go to another place
And the people never caused a stir, by saying
They didn't want it there; they just let it be.
Their Sphinx still looks out across the sand
In Egypt, and our iron men gaze out to sea
In another place.
The Sphinx is interesting, but then, I much
Prefer the iron men, and in a way;
I'm inclined to think that they should stay
But allow me to allay your fears,
I don't mean for three thousand years.

Rosemary Osa Quirke

THE DYING GIUSEPPE MAZZIN

Eyes closed, hands folded
Lying on his bed,
Thinking of what, when, why,
He knows he'll soon be dead.

Loves lost memories faded,
Life's become jaded,
Scores settled, affairs in order,
Time to meet with heaven's warder.

Don't be sad please don't cry,
Everyone has to die,
Don't be angry please don't shout,
The sands of time will soon run out.

My heart's slowed down,
My breath's ran out,
It's almost time to bow out,
I've lived my life and had some fun,
Do the same, enjoy it son.

Edward Marriette

FIRST VISITOR

Mam! He's like uncle Fred!
He takes after his dad!
When he smiles he's got our Mary's dimple
He's not smiling. That's wind!

Then he's got the wind bad. He knows I'm his sister! It's simple,
What a love, what a pet, mam, can't I hold him yet?
How d'you know he's a boy? Can I see?

No, you can't! You're too rough, covered in chocolate stuff

Well, we went to McDonald's for tea
One cuddle won't harm him, my face can't alarm him,
It's milkshake and babies like milk,
His fingers are clutching, that's my thumb he's touching,
His hair is so soft, mam, like silk.

What's that horrible smell? Is it him? I'nt he well?
Here, you'd better take him, instead,
Yuk! I feel sick, get his nappy off, quick!

All babies do that, don't be silly!

Did I poo green slime?
Did I cry all the time?
Mam, why haven't I got a willy?

Rosemary Critchley

A POEM OF CARRICKFERGUS

Carrickfergus is home to me,
Situated on Belfast sea.
With white harbour peering out.
Breaking sea horses from its spout.
This famous town on Fergus rock
Has a castle and a clock.
This norman fort, is tall and strong,
A castle extremely tall and long.
In the town there is a wall,
Built of stone to surround us all.
As we head north to Jacksons site
We think of all his power and might.
Time in Fergus will always be
A special place for you and me.
As I look out at sunset west
We have a hill full of quest.
So when you pass or fly by
Please stop and hear my seagulls cry.

Shauna Grant

PORTAVOGIE

Along the peninsula down by the sea
Is a wee small village that is home to me
It doesn't have much for the big city man
But its peaceful tranquillity suits me just grand.

It has no shopping centres with big flashy lights
Or the hustle and bustle you find with these sights
Pollutants in the air with cars passing by
People on the streets in the dead of the night.

It has rolling countryside with fields of green
Cows gently lowing where the air is fresh and clean
Red autumn sunsets caressing golden fields of wheat
Farmers on the land tending their sheep.

A leisurely stroll and you're down by the shore
Watching the fishing boats return home once more
Skillfully mending nets when their time is free
So they can catch fish for you and me

Fiona J Finegan

DRESSOG DAYS

Dressog days and Dressog braes, each one I used to know
Dressog times, I left behind, so many years ago
Dressog hills, I would climb to yellow flowered whin bushes
By Dressog meadows I did hide deep among the rushes

In Dressog bogs, I'd catch some frogs and put them into
jars
Beside Dressog streams, I'd often dream, beneath the stars
Up Dressog lanes, in the pouring rain I'd shelter by a tree
And when the weather was dry under a Dressog sky, I'd
roam the countryside, so free

In Dressog fields, I can reveal, I spent so many happy
hours
On a summer's day, I would play among the lovely flowers,
Along Dressog roads, I used to stroll as the sun was sink-
ing, in the west
Those Dressog days, now gone away, they were the very
best.

Patrick Gormley

THE COTTAGE

There's an old and derelict cottage
The place where we called home
Just three miles north of Cookstown
On the border of County Tyrone

Mother's songs rang out through the window
As she baked our griddle bread
Watching out for the children's safety
Making sure we all were fed

Beautiful cottage you're silent now
Your walls so steady and strong
So many families you've seen pass away
Sadly six members of our own have passed along

Stand still and watch for us all coming back
We'll be searching to see you again
For more of us may have to leave you awhile
Through death, sickness and pain

Joseph Mullan

MAGUIRES BRIDGE THE TUG-OF-WAR TEAM

Every man had played his part
And never faltered from the start.
Feet well anchored for a better grip
With hob nail boots that will not slip.

Strong hands tighten around the rope
Every man must now have hope.
A victory here they can achieve
When Gavan calls on all to heave.

The pulling starts, there's sweat and pain
Not an inch does either gain
All of a sudden, things look great
The bridge is winning, it's not too late.

This war they'll win, they all believe
When Gavan calls, another heave.
One final pull from this team of men
And Maguires bridge have won again.

Vincent Breen

A LESSON IN GOODNESS

Awfully awkward Alfred, the product of a slum
Born and bred in Shankill, a docker's only son.
Steeped in grave religion, a faith strong and true
His arms of workers' muscles, his ideas firm as glue.
No pious resolutions from the pompous prophet's tongue
Will stir his heart strings or drive him from the union of the
orange or the blue.

It was in a pub I met him, *will ye have a pint?* says I
Ah ye dirty scheming papist you're tempting me to sin,
I'll have a pint of Guinness, he piped up with a grin.
He downed it with a gargle and proceeded to pronounce
By God you know them Fenians must have credit for that
brew.

So perhaps here lies the answer for the north and for the
south
For who can talk of hatred from behind a pint of stout,
And then we'll live together as the bitterness it rots
United by the goodness in a hundred thousand hops.

Mark Long

DISAPPEAR

Hear the whispers,
Through the mountains,
Singing a song,
Lost in the day.

Ships sailing at night,
But where do they go?
Swallowed by the sea,
While white horses play.

Empty voices,
Scream in silence,
Under the moon,
Under the stars.

Julie Parker

Julie Parker said: "I am a new author/illustrator. I have
been writing poetry since I was a child and have always
loved the way words can create such a powerful feeling. I
was born on the 22nd November 1983 and have always
had a great passion for all areas of the arts. I have recently
graduated with a Bachelor's Degree in Illustration from
University College, Falmouth. Please visit my website
www.julieillustration.co.uk or email me with any comments
on this poem as I would love to hear from you."

THE HISTORICAL METHOD

I have moved many times
But will always return
I've commenced many trials
But will always adjourn
I am tied somehow
With ne'er a pardon
To a certain locale
In history's back garden
It's here that I grew
'Twixt the road and the field
Despite my objection
To memory I yield
There is no distinction
Between then and now
Age doesn't concern me
To a time lag I bow
Though I often falter
Clearly I see
To remain local
Is my final decree

Keith Watson

MY LAGAN LOCK

Here I sit and reminisce
Looking back on childhood bliss
Recalling times of long ago
With barges going to and fro
Carrying goods and coal galore
A ride once given I did adore
A horse it pulled the heavy load
Water transport was then a mode
Maisie, Betty, Bill or Saul
Names of horses one may recall
Some barges even had family life
The owner living with child and wife
Keepers of the lock came out
When boatmen gave a bellowing shout
The water level he now did lower
Then opened up the great big door
On it went at steady pace
To journey on the horse did face
No barges now for man to fill
This lock it brings back memories still

Harry Press

COUNTY DOWN

Her beauty spots are world-renowned
So here each year many visitors have found
There are lots of things to see and do
A real hearty welcome and great food too.
Now how about visiting to see for yourself
What God gave us - A glorious wealth

You'll find the Mourne Mountains ideal for a hike
Stroll on Newcastle's beach or swim if you like
There are many golf courses also boating for pleasure
Three Councils provide sports complexes for leisure
There are racecourses for horses, motorbikes and cars
Football and cricket matches that go on for hours

Also National Trust estates, I'll name but a few
Castle Ward and Mount Stewart are all open to view
There is Scrabo Tower and statues depicting our history
Stories and folklore to unravel their mystery
A handicraft industry, home produces galore
So you'll find unique presents for friends to adore

Georgina Wright

THE WORKHOUSE

Like a giant grey ghost on a mound it protrudes
Reminder of famine and ration of food
In stillness of night it echoes inside
Of rumbling bellies where man gave up and died
For want of food men left barren land
Because of landlords greed and outstretched hands
Many a soul left bodies to rest at the side of the road before
it was blessed
In 1842 it opened it's doors where our ancestors sheltered
from the elements fuels
They dined on potatoes morning and night
'Til the famine crept in with a thief called the blight
Crops all died like poison on weed
Then inmates were fed on Indian meal
In 1846 two days a week they had treats of molasses, rice
and sweet milk
Now the iron pot in its retired state rests at the back just
inside the gate
If you ever pass by bow your head and your knee
For inmates of the workhouse in Lisnaskea

Anna McBrien

CARRICKFERGUS

A place where I was born,
Where I've grown,
A place I call home!
I feel Carrick is underrated, look around you!
A leisure centre, complete with a pool,
A museum, filled with facts, statistics and history!
The Castle, Carrick's very own landmark,
A harbour, marina and shops galore,
Why do people keep wanting more?
In Carrick, life's good - a town to brighten the mood!
At thirteen, I've witnessed changes,
New shops, change in the colour of the flower beds, new
cinema and *the knight ride.*
A place to hang out with mates, have a laugh and have a
chat,
When I take a visit, what I plan is exactly that.
If people would just open their eyes,
And take a minute to look around,
They'd realise they live in a great town!
I love Carrick, it's full of history,
And to call it home, makes me proud,
We even have a yellow Town Hall!

Emma Murray

BELFAST

Through years of strife and trouble
A City bruised but not thrown down
Building for a new tomorrow
Hoping for a bright new dawn
Kind, friendly, helpful people
Across a deep divide
Building ships and aircraft
Our City can be proud

Famous White Star liners
Sailing into history's page
From the shadow of the gantries
Beneath the Atlantic's wave
The Island Yard deserted now
Samson and Goliath stand
A silent witness to the men
Who built these liners grand

May Belfast City see the day
When friendship's hand shall reach
From East to West o'er Lagan's wave
The uniting bond of peace

Winston Graydon

BONEYBEFORE

East of Eden, on Belfast Loughs' shore,
Lies the little village of Boneybefore.

It was named by travellers and coach drivers of yore,
This beautiful village of Boneybefore.
On their journeys from Larne, to Belfast town,
In this little canton they bedded down.

In a white washed, thatched cottage
Stonewall Jackson was conceived,
And over the years its name was abbreviated.

The bonny village before Carrick
On Belfast's Lough shore,
Over the years became Boneybefore.

Lying east of Eden with sands like ripe corn,
And in the distance, the mountains of Mourne.

It is so steeped in history
With tourists galore,
This beautiful village of Boneybefore.

Shirley Gault

AUTUMN

I gaze out towards the Lough shore
Watching as the gale strips the trees
And chases racing waves across
The stony grey surface of the shallows.
Leaves lie dying, beautiful in their demise,
Under a streaked sky, void of birds.
Shafts of strong sunlight break through
To cast dark shadows on the fields.
A moment, a window on creation
Order, variety, majesty on show,
As I pause to notice
The handiwork of God.

Rhonda Todd

CARRICKFERGUS

Carrickfergus by the sea,
Such a beautiful place to be,
It is perfect, just for me,
Carrickfergus by the sea.

Carrickfergus by the sea,
Ancient castle, lots to see,
Fishermen at Fisherman's quay,
Carrickfergus by the sea.

Carrickfergus by the sea,
Parks and playgrounds, beautiful trees,
Falling leaves and stormy seas,
Carrickfergus by the sea.

Aimee Hislop

THE WALLACE MONUMENT

Established high upon a hill, if you're nearby you can see,
This mighty rock standing still, it's surely not considered
wee

Steeped in local history, tribute to a famous man,
Who made his enemies flee and fought to save his trea-
sured land.

The city that was once a town, industrial and cultured.
This shrine every day looks down. The view again has
altered.

Tourists come to see the tower but do they see real life?
Or the actors strength and power when brandishing a
knife?

The steps that lead you to the top are worth the long, steep
climb.
When you finally sit and stop you'll want to spend more
time.

This is where I changed my life just four months ago.
Where I agreed to be a wife whilst looking down below.

Gillian Ewing

HEALING ILLUSION

Home is where the heart's torn out
All healing spurned our efforts turned
Towards a game of claim and blame.
A time of change? Much still the same,
Save where our endless curse grows worse.

Home is where hollow heroes shout,
Drowning wisdom's whisper, sure to prosper
By preaching tolerance, practising hate.
Rival flags, like rags the bulls to bait
Fly poles apart, one man's demon, another's heart.

Home, we're told is what it's all about,
Blood it's price, greed its vice,
Present and future slaves to the past.
Who sinned first and who'll laugh last?
Revenge and possession our abiding obsession.

Home is a place with no room for doubt,
All certain sure our causes are pure,
Accusations our chief stock in trade.
With faces as long as our famed Lurgan spade,
We dig in and languish in our trenches.

Paul Wilkinson

WHICH WAY?

From Dundonald village to Newtownards town by the busy
dual carriageway,
Or shall I take the the winding road on this bright autum-
nal day?
Two places so different in which to be,
The hustle bustle of the town, or the beauty of the country.

Here in Killynether wood in the autumn mornings misty
dim,
Tree skeletons appear tall and thin.
Leaves reddening, pale amber, yellow and brown,
Carpet the wood's earthy floor as they flutter down.
Climbing to a viewpoint high,
On a hill stands Scrabo Tower like a finger pointing
towards the sky.
There it stands in its majesty,
Below Strangford Lough ebbs out towards the sea.
The drumlins and farms of Ards countryside, fields with
sheep, cows and the last bales of hay.
The Mourne Mountains dominate the skyline faraway.
Cyclists riding down quiet country lanes.
Over the hills, Belfast's shipyard, Titanic's birthplace and
famous cranes.

Florence Bradshaw

MALIN HEAD TO FAIR HEAD

The beauty that lies between these two
is much too much to miss,
because it is there for all to see
and for the tourists' bliss.

There is the Foyle so wide and fair
that flows out past the Point,
where the ferry joins two ports just now
that make their people more *joint.*

Benone with beach so clean and grand,
Downhill to Castlerock,
on to the *Ports* with all their beauty,
one can't but else take stock.

The Whiterocks and Giant's Causeway
are gorgeous no matter the weather,
God gave the Causeway as our own true *Wonder*
make the effort and see it together.

On to Bushmills with distillery there,
the Carrick-a-Rede Rope Bridge must be seen,
whilst Fair Head may be the last to mention
this completes a most majestic scene.

Raymond Meenagh

OLE TIPPERARY

You would find him at the corner of any street, he looked
always neat, or dancing to his own words of Danny Boy, he
was full of life and oozing joy.
His long dark woolly coat, his black hair swept back with
the brillcream shine.
And from his pocket peeping through a half bottle of
Mundies wine.

Everyone knew this harmless man.
A gentleman with manners, compassion and love, but drink
was his master, unfortunately so.

It created this character and destroyed him too.
It cut his life short.
His name no one forgets.
Known to all in our wee town, remembered by all without a
frown
Harmless soul, may he rest in peace, for yet his stories are
still told by all the old
That saluted ole tip, that's Tipperary.

Regina McLaughlin

Born in Derry, **Regina McLaughlin** has interests including
writing, poetry and short stories. "I would love to write on a
professional level and my work is influenced by my mother,
husband and children," she explained. "I worked as a credit
controller and recently retired after 29 years of service."
Regina is married to Charles and they have sons Richard,
Christopher and Jordan. "I have written several poems and
have had three published," added Regina.

BANBRIDGE

Banbridge - town on river Bann,
Where tired or eager eyes can scan
Places of beauty - nature's plan,
Or gaze in awe at skill of man.

The *cut* with stout walls aged and grey,
Mellowed with echoes of stagecoach sway,
Old linen mills that once did boom,
With fly of shuttle and swing of loom.

The parish church with noble steeple,
Monuments to famous people,
Writers, sculptors, gallant men,
Renowned for deed or sweep of pen.

A market town whose roads outreach,
To city fair or sandy beach,
To forest park and rolling hill,
To quiet lake or babbling rill.

The lyric's home of famous girl,
A precious stone or cultured pearl,
A coloured shawl round pretty gown,
Banbridge, star of County Down.

Joan C Fyvie

BREATH OF DAWN

From the mountain to the Glen,
Distant memories does she send,
For from us now she is gone,
On the wings of eagles - on the breath of dawn.

My best friend was her true love,
And married we thought they'd be,
But no one is promised tomorrow,
What will be will always be.

Quick she was to anger,
But always first to smile,
Her language strong as her blue eyes shone,
But still an innocent child.

Our days she laced with laughter,
Our nights she spiced with song,
And she and I were guilty,
Of just a little wrong!

Her laughter seems so fresh now,
As I lay down to rest,
God's garden must be beautiful,
For he only picks the best.

John Matthew Jamison

MY AREA

I live in a peaceful place,
Where the wind is crisp and light,
Where the scent of the flowers is so aromatic,
Where the sun is oh so bright.

Where the hills and streams hold hands,
Where the birds sing many a tune,
Where the trees blow through the air,
Where the stars sit by the moon.

Where crops of wheat are grown,
Where greenery thrives all year,
Where clouds are high and fluffy,
Where nature has no fear.

Where azure skies are familiar,
Where rabbits frolic and leap,
Where birds build nests out of twigs,
Where cows wander with sheep.

This place is heaven for wildlife,
So undisturbed and calm,
A quiet little place near Magherafelt,
Ballyriff is the town land.

Bernadette Kevin

ARTIST

A scrawl of branches,
Bare and black,
Etch their thin outlines against
The pewter palette of the sky;
The eye of heaven weeps
For the lost year,
While the grey ghost of winter
Haunts the hills and chills
The bleak bones of beech
And birch and oak.

Betty McIlroy

BELFAST BOY

Belfast boy, with those azure eyes
and the print of God's thumb in your chin
beneath that dazzling smile
you captured our hearts.
You were poetry in motion
on those weaving dancing feet
world icon, our boy, blessed with genius
with Mercury's wings on your heels.
Now a swaying ribbon of grief
weeps along with heaven's tears
as sweet voices ease your passage home.
Even in death, you seduce us
as you are carried high
crowned by fragrant lilies,
and then are laid to rest
in the soft brown earth,
Belfast boy, safe
in your mother's arms.

Joan MacCabe

THE ANTRIM COAST

When the weather is fine and I've nothing to do,
I head for the coast to savour the view
of the cliffs and the glens of the Antrim hills
and to stop by the pools that the waterfalls fill.

I see the rope bridge and the Giant's Causeway,
Then I head for the arch o'er the road at Redbay.
I visit the village of old Cushendall,
where folks enjoy rounds with a golf club and ball.

The Island of Rathlin where Robert the Bruce
watched the cave spider's web six times break loose,
Is plain to be seen not far from the shore,
where Marconi's remembered for evermore.

I drive to Carnlough where the home made ice-cream
is tasty enough to serve to a Queen.
I watch the men in the harbour there,
tying their boats to the pier with care.

When I've travelled the road from Portrush to Larne,
I stop for a while to have a good yarn
with the man who believes in the fairy tree.
Then I head back again to my home for tea.

Daniel Shaw

THE DRAY HORSE

I see you as you are today
Like an engine, without a soul
And think you once shared meadows sweet
A sturdy frolicking foal.

But then you were taken far away
Did they take your manhood too
Your time for rest now concrete stalls
With others just like you.

Your days here spent by city docks
Haul carts up to the flat
Traffic, noise, surrounds blanked out
Has your life now come to that.

Big bony legs and body lean
Years shaped you with the load
When once your head and ears held high
Today they're near the road.

They'll work you till they'll say you're done
Too old and stiff for gain
Please be it when they cull you off
You'll see meadows once again.

William Donaldson

BANBRIDGE

I relish in borne from the *Kingdom of Mourne*
as I rest on the banks of the Bann.
Where Colleens of dreams grace every scene,
from the Yellow Hill' through Ballyvalley townland.

A tunnel of vision, bestowed near my heart,
Gives me heritage not to disown,
As did my green fields in grace, once ornately dressed
With linen pure from the loom.

While a great son in birth blessed,
In honour dispersed, his love for the Son Of God.
Another in his plight, gave his young life
As he searched for the *Passage North-West.*

Reluctant I am to unfair demand
In peace time in war time or woe.
Within my sequential scene, my sons find their dream
And in contentment I bloom in North Ireland.

Through autumn to winter, in fiery colour I dress.
In springtime I bloom with the rose.
With blue skies or grey I meet every new day,
Worthy I am of any poet's prose.

Elizabeth Aulds

THE ISLAND OF ENNISKILLEN

In the South of Fermanagh lies the town of Enniskillen
Situated between two bridges, a wonderful scene.
It holds much history, Maguire the clan:
Despite many battles, castle ruins still stand.

Surrounded by green pastures and waters blue,
Hundreds of boats sail there, old and new.
Lough Erne holds the honour - Devenish Island, so serene,
peaceful and tranquil, Oh what a dream.

Throughout all seasons, where we are free to roam
On the edge of Enniskillen, there is a stately home.
Encircled by beautiful landscapes, Castlecoole is its name
Highly recommended for walks and its fame.

The lakes are a magnet for fishermen, far and near
Entering many competitions and sorting their gear
Then to the pub for the craic and the Guinness
Music, songs and laughter, with many to finish.

Sir Lowry Cole's monument towers high above the town
108 steps there are to climb
A stunning view of the finest kind
Picturesque Fermanagh, a jewel in the Crown.

Mona Sharkey

LIMAVADY

The town of Limavady
Is famous in many ways.
It has seen a lot of changes
Since the bygone days.

With the River Roe along its side,
The making of *The Derry Air,*
Lads have come from near and far
To court the lasses oh so fair.

There was blind fiddler Jimmy McCurry
And Jane Ross, the music player too,
Not forgetting William Massey,
That's only some of the chosen few.

There are shops, houses, schools and all
And lots of churches there,
In November every year
There was the *Gallop Fair*

And now I've told you a little
Of history here, so when,
My twenty lines are finished,
I must put down the pen.

Olive Thompson

CLONKEEN

In Gaelic it means Pleasant Meadow
This townland of Clonkeen,
It lies just outside Randalstown
Beside Lough Neagh to set the scene.

I've lived in these here parts
For just over ten years now,
But there's always been a connection
It's uncanny, don't ask me how.

Perhaps it's my obsession
For historical facts and folklore.
This place was planted by the settlers,
And was the O'Neills of Shane's Castle before.

In years gone by a tenant farmer
Leased an acre or two of bog,
And a single room thatched cottage
Gave shelter to six kids, a wife and a dog.

All the family ate was potatoes
To ward off hunger and disease,
But consumption was a killer
It had the community on its knees.

Church yards still contain the headstones
Of young children who didn't survive.
Looking back has a useful purpose,
It makes you glad to be alive.

Pauline Herbison

A FERMANAGH ARTIST

Michael was born an artist,
A talent before he could walk.
An ear for traditional music,
Mick Hoy made the auld fiddle talk.

He played at Fleadhs all over Ireland,
In pubs and out on the street,
His footsteps were light, a gentleman true,
As old friends and new he would greet.

In homesteads he played in the corner,
As the turf fire lit up the room,
Head tilted in posing he'd squint and nod,
Sure I'll play you a bit of a tune.

The people were gathered and merry,
They'd cheer in laughter and shout.
Placed on the fallen leaf table,
Mick's occasional bottle of stout.

He rang in the year 2000,
Celebrated the new century,
God must have wanted a fiddler,
We just had to let it be.

Music was played at his graveside,
Respect and honour to rest,
Fermanagh's finest fiddle player,
Remembered as one of the best.

Marian McGrath

IMAGINE

Imagine! there's a great wee town
With lots of shops indeed.
It's convenient and compatible for everybody's needs.
Tea shops, paper shops, clothes shops more,
Look around our centre for merchandise galore.
Supermarkets, garages, chemists and parks,
Streets where you don't even hear dogs bark.
Buses, taxis, coach or train,
All of these amenities in our wee town Coleraine.

Margaret Smyth

FORGOTTEN WORLD

The world is so beautiful
The world is so beautiful
I'm looking into the heart of God

The world is so beautiful
His love is irreplaceable
His heart is shaping me

The world is so beautiful
The world is so beautiful
So come and tell me I'm not real

The world is so beautiful
Its change is inevitable
The world is so beautiful

Despite everything I can see

Charlene Ramsey

STORMONT'S VIEW

Crisp autumnal air, white breath evaporating
Fading light
Beyond lies the silhouetted cityscape
A soft red haze entwined in mist
Rustling leaves in a cool breeze - a touch of winters hand
Bare finger-like branches, naked, cold alone
Street lights flicker to call us home
A longing for home comforts, security, warmth
The snap of twigs and leaves beneath
Above the city the moon lights up its dark places
Shining from a far away place - out there - beyond us -
only its face is hidden by fleeting clouds
Night falls quickly and darkness descends
The curtain is lowered and another day ends

Sharon Proctor

NO DRESS

My city
Will wear no dress
It will not sparkle with diamonds
Instead
It will wear
The wind and the trees
It will not invite you
To a ball with closed doors
Instead
It will show you
How to dance
With the sound of the sea
In your ears
The beautiful hum
Of the world around you
This is a city of intervention
A dancer with the wind

Jean Gardner

LURGAN

There's nothing poetic about Lurgan,
No beauty to be seen;
This is the town that fathered a child
And abandoned it in between.

Sulky shops stagger from pillar to post;
They're shuttered for sale on each dice's roll.
Banks offer loans but easily foreclose,
Forcing death on the people's soul.

So, apathetic, pathetic,
Bored shoulders bowed,
All eyes are down
Boring the ground,
Betting on the hound of opportunity;
Prophets of doom profiting by loss.

They spay territorial claims on street corners,
Picking at scabs so healing never comes.
The scene is one of closure,
But underneath it's never been close;
They spade the hole for their own burial.

Kittie Carr

LIMAVADY

My home town is Limavady
A grand *wee* place to know
I cycled there and back each day
Now I'm ninety years and four

I have seen so many changes
I wouldn't know just where to start
In my young days cars were few
Most folk went by horse and cart

It's known as *The Roe Valley*
With its lovely River Roe
The Londonderry air was made there
But sadly the hospital is no more

The town is so much bigger now
The older shops are no more
The streets are one way system
Compared to days of yore

I could recall a whole lot more
But as this is verse number five
I'll take a rest from poet's corner
And just thank God I'm still alive

Ella Stirling

HELEN'S BAY

When your fight's in vain.
On the heavy day
I would take the train,
Come to Helen's Bay.

Dig my fingers deep
Into flowing sand.
With the winds I'll weep,
Wait for tears to end.

I will wipe my face,
Watch the waves and follow.
Loose myself in space
Since the heart is hollow.

Swap my blood that boils
For the salt in veins.
Leave the love that spoils,
Wash away the pains.

Swallow, swallow me
Highest, youngest tide,
Strong and carefree
Take me all inside...

Natalia Tochenykh

FAMOUS BANBRIDGE TOWN

There were many famous people who from Banbridge town
have come,
And when I stroll through Solitude it makes me think of
some
Did Rawdon Crozier once walk here in days of long ago
And did memory bring him home again while battling in
the snow.

Helen Waddle loved this town, or so I have been told
A famous scholar of her time, her name now written in gold
And Joseph Scriven of great fame much loved until the end
He wrote a universal hymn when Jesus was his friend.

And of its young folk here I say there's good in every heart
And very good potential here to set themselves apart
To bring more fame to Banbridge with that already made
With my spirit free I'd love to see the ones who make the
grade.

Peggy Galloway

THE POOL OF LIFE

As the Liverbirds watch over the city.
The derby begins and the fans cheer or cry in pity.
As Everton loses and Liverpool wins!
How lovely now is the Albert Dock,
From the Tate to The Beatles to the yellow duck.
To the summer pops the fans all flock.
As the sun sets over the river,
Ferry cross the Mersey, you're never far from home.
When you live in Liverpool you never walk alone.

Sally Evans

Full Colour

Stephen King, Mark Twain, Lord Byron, George Bernard Shaw, Beatrix Potter, Jane Austen, Rudyard Kipling and Edgar Allen Poe were just a few of the writers who began their careers by contributing to their publication costs. So, if you decide to produce your own book, you are in elevated company.

Thanks to new technology you can now even print your own poetry book with a full colour cover, starting at just £267. (Or only £168 in black and white onto marble card).

You can select your colour cover from a wide range of dazzling images which can be viewed by visiting our website at *www.unitedpress.co.uk*. If you don't have a computer you can go to your local library or internet cafe to see the images.

When you go onto the website click on *publications* then click on *book covers*. This will allow you to view all the many covers which you can choose from. Or you can provide your own photo or painting.

United Press produces everything from books of poetry to novels in a variety of covers including softback and hardback. Just telephone 0870 240 6190 and we will put details and a free sample in the post to you straight away.

For all writers, getting into print is the pinnacle of ambition. Thanks to United Press you now have that ambition easily within your reach.

❏ *You can also visit our website to find out about the charity work done by United Press.*